FOOTBALL CONDITIONING
A MODERN SCIENTIFIC APPROACH

PERIODIZATION | SEASONAL TRAINING | SMALL SIDED GAMES

Written by

Adam Owen, Ph.D

(Assistant Author: Alexandre Dellal, Ph.D)

Published by

FOOTBALL CONDITIONING
A MODERN SCIENTIFIC APPROACH

PERIODIZATION | SEASONAL TRAINING | SMALL SIDED GAMES

First Published August 2016 by SoccerTutor.com
Info@soccertutor.com | www.SoccerTutor.com

UK: 0208 1234 007 | **US:** (305) 767 4443 | **ROTW:** +44 208 1234 007

ISBN: 978-1-910491-10-2

Author

Adam Owen, Ph.D

Assistant Author

Alexandre Dellal, Ph.D

Edited by

Alex Fitzgerald - SoccerTutor.com

Cover Design by

Alex Macrides, Think Out Of The Box Ltd.
Email: design@thinkootb.com Tel: +44 (0) 208 144 3550

Infographic Design by

Yann Le Meur; @YLMSportScience
(Images for infographics provided by Presenter Media, USA)

Photography by

Willie Vass Photography, Glasgow and Propaganda Photography, Liverpool

Diagrams

Diagram designs by SoccerTutor.com. All the diagrams in this book have been created using SoccerTutor.com Tactics Manager Software available from www.SoccerTutor.com

Note: While every effort has been made to ensure the technical accuracy of the content of this book, neither the author nor publishers can accept any responsibility for any injury or loss sustained as a result of the use of this material.

CONTENTS

MEET THE AUTHOR

Dr. Adam Owen

 @adamowen1980

 www.aoperformance.co.uk

Credentials:

- UEFA Professional Coaching Licence
  (Football Association of Wales (FAW), Cardiff)

- Doctor of Philosophy (Ph.D) in Sport and Exercise Science
  (Claude Bernard Lyon.1 University, Lyon, France)

- Master of Philosophy (M.Phil) Degree in Sport and Exercise
  (Glyndwr University, Wrexham, Wales, UK)

- BSc (HONS) Degree in Sport and Exercise Science
  (Glyndwr University, Wrexham, Wales, UK)

Current and Previous Coaching Roles:

- Wales National Team Sport Science and Fitness Coach

- Football Research Scientist Consultant at SL Benfica, Lisbon, Portugal

- Assistant Coach and Head of Performance at Servette FC, Switzerland

- Associate Research Scientist at Claude Bernard Lyon.1 University, France

- Visiting Academic at the Technological and Higher Education Institute
  (THEi), Hong Kong

- Head of Fitness and Performance at Sheffield United FC, England

- Head of Sport Science and Performance at Rangers FC, Scotland

- Head of Fitness and Science at Sheffield Wednesday FC, England

- Head of Sport Science at Celtic FC Academy, Scotland

- Technical and Fitness Coach at Wrexham FC Academy, Wales

Additional Information:

Throughout his career, Adam Owen has developed a unique blend of practical coaching experience (UEFA Pro Coaching Licence holder) with the development of a very prominent and active academic profile, obtaining a Ph.D in the field of Sport Science and Coaching (Lyon.1 University, France). In addition to this, he is a very active coach educator and is involved within many research projects throughout the world of 'football science'.

Experiencing many roles within the game (i.e. playing, coaching, sport science and high performance implementation), Adam has been able to combine his practical and scientific understanding, thoughts and experiences gained within the game at a range of professional levels to form a philosophy outlined in this book.

Adam's career has seen him progress from elite youth level to senior level across domestic football, European campaigns (UEFA Champions League and Europa League), European club football and elite level International football (UEFA European Championships and FIFA World Cup qualification campaigns).

He has been able to utilise previous European and domestic success to develop a justifiable, research based coaching method in order to maximise individual and group performance within elite professional football. The focussed integration of all key technical, sport science and medical personnel is something that ensures best practice in the constant evolving football industry.

At the age of 27 Adam was part of the Rangers FC senior management staff who reached a major European Cup Final and went on implement a successful 'football science' department, remaining at the club for a long period of time.

In the summer of 2014, Adam accepted the opportunity to move to European club football in order to further experience the challenges of working abroad in the central belt of Europe whilst continuing his work with the senior Wales national team. Adam continues to review, write and publish scientific journal articles and book chapters, whilst acting as an Associate Researcher for Claude Bernard Lyon.1 University in France and holds a consultancy role as a Research Scientist at SL Benfica in Portugal.

ASSISTANT AUTHOR

Dr. Alexandre Dellal

Credentials:

- UEFA 'A' Coaching Licence
  (French Football Federation [F.F.F], Clairefontaine)

- Doctor of Philosophy (Ph.D) in Sport Science
  (University of Strasbourg, France)

- DEA Research Master Degree
  (University of Nancy-Strasbourg 2, France)

- DESS Master Course in Physical Preparation
  (University of Strasbourg, France)

Current and Previous Coaching Roles:

- Head of Physical Preparation, OGC Nice, France

- Research Scientist, FIFA Medical Centre of Excellence, Centre Orthopédique
  Santy, Lyon, France

- Head Fitness Coach, Olympique Lyonnais, France

- Fitness Coach, Ivory Coast National Football Team, Ivory Coast, Africa

- Head of Sport Rehabilitation, Cryonic Medical, France

- Fitness Coach, Al Ittihad, Jeddah, Saudi Arabia

Throughout the content of the book, Dr. Dellal contributed significantly within the various chapters using his extensive research knowledge, in addition to his practical application skills to assist in making the transition to the coaching link.

Dr. Alexandre Dellal is one of the most highly regarded football research scientists within the game. He is currently Head of Physical Preparation at French Ligue 1 side OGC Nice, whilst also holding a research position at FIFA Medical Center of Excellence, Centre Orthopédique Santy in Lyon, France. He currently holds the UEFA 'A' Coaching Licence and received a Ph.D from Lyon.1 University in France within the area of sport science and coaching where he continues to be an Associate Researcher.

He was previously at Olympique Lyonnais as Head of Physical Preparation and has also worked at International level with the Ivory Coast National team throughout their successful African Cup of Nations period. A very active researcher in the field of sport and football science, he has numerous scientific journal publications, books and on-going research projects.

Other Acknowledgments and Research Collaborators

Shane Malone (Training Load and Monitoring): RISES Liverpool John Moores University, Liverpool, UK.

Dr. Mehdi Rouissi (Injury Prevention): National Centre of Medicine and Science in Sports, Tunis, Tunisia.

Prof. Karim Chamari (Injury Prevention and Physiology): Scientific Researcher, Aspetar, Qatar.

Prof. Del P. Wong (Physiology): Sport Science Research Centre, Shandong University, China.

Willie Vass Photography | Glasgow | UK
Propaganda Photography | Liverpool | UK
Yann Le Meur Infographics | @YLMSportScience | Monaco | France

REFERENCES

Aaron Ramsey

Arsenal Football Club and Wales National Team Player

"Having known and worked with Adam for many years at International level, he is someone I enjoy working with and have benefited in many areas of my game due to his methods and knowledge. I look forward to working with him for many years to come."

Steven Davis

Southampton Football Club and Northern Ireland National Team Captain

"Adam and I worked together for many years during a significant and successful part of my career. His knowledge in his specialised area, and the philosophy he implemented from a science and performance aspect within the club was excellent. As a result, it led to an improvement in me as a professional."

Prof. Karim Chamari

Scientific Researcher Aspetar, Qatar

"The detail within this particular book is of great interest to both scientific researchers and applied practitioners who are keen to develop their knowledge from both perspectives. Having collaborated on many research projects and publications, Adam has a very impressive practical profile in addition to continually developing his sound research background in applied sport and coaching science. This is highlighted within this book as I feel it shows a direct relationship, linking both areas."

Prof. Del P. Wong

Sport Science Research Center, Shandong Sport University, China

"Having collaborated with Adam for nearly 10 years on numerous sport science developments (mainly football science research), one of his main strengths is the ability to link cutting edge science to the on-field performance to stimulate a different thought process as highlighted throughout this book. Attaining the UEFA Pro Coaching Licence and a Ph.D degree, is a rare but very impressive combination which make him very unique in our field. The information provided within this book highlights the link between the science and on-pitch coaching structure."

Football Conditioning: A Modern Scientific Approach

FOREWORD BY WALTER SMITH

Walter Smith OBE

Manager at Rangers FC, Everton FC, Scotland National Team and Assistant Manager at Manchester United FC

"Over recent years, the role of science to assist in player development and subsequent increased performance at the top level has grown stronger. This particular book discusses the progressive link between physical development, coaching principles, coach education and player preparation.

Individuals involved within the education and delivery processes of the game, at a range of levels, will enjoy the content of this book and be able to integrate some key findings within their coaching structure. For the reader, the book outlines the physical, technical and subsequent link to the tactical demands imposed upon professional football players in both training and competitive games. In order to execute a particular tactical game plan at any level, teams must be capable of physically performing within the tactical approach adopted for the duration of the game.

The contemporary approach of the book focusses on the training session design and clear justifications for specific methods employed within the modern game. Maximising the link between the technical, tactical and physical aspect of the game has seen an increased use of technology, analysis and specific personnel within a range of roles to ensure performance levels are maximised, and player injury is minimised. As a result, this book encapsulates these topics and highlights the fact that Adam is one of the most innovative performance coaches, underpinning sound football specific practice with scientific knowledge.

The key coaching messages within the chapters ensure an easy to follow strategy can be implemented. The philosophy employed and the role he played as part of my management staff played a major part in our achievements both in domestic and European competition."

KEY TERMS

- **Adenosine Triphosphate (ATP):** is the energy currency of life. ATP is a high-energy molecule found in every cell. Its job is to store and supply the cell with needed energy.

- **Aerobic:** Exercise performed to improve the use, absorption and transportation of oxygen around the body.

- **Aerobic Capacity:** The highest amount of oxygen consumed during maximal exercise in activities.

- **Anaerobic:** Exercise that is fuelled primarily without the use oxygen.

- **Anaerobic Capacity:** Short duration exercise periods that are primarily powered without the use of oxygen. These movements or activities produce high lactate levels.

- **Anaerobic Metabolism:** The creation of energy through the combustion of carbohydrates and fats in the presence of oxygen. The only by-products are carbon dioxide and water, which your body disposes of by breathing and sweating.

- **bLa (Blood Lacate):** Lactic acid that appears within the blood as a result of oxygen delivery to the working muscles being insufficient to support the work performed.

- **Cardiac Output (Q):** The amount of blood the heart can pump through the circulatory system in a minute.

- **Circadian Rhythms:** Daily rhythmic activity cycle based on 24 hour intervals.

- **COD:** Change of direction.

- **Creatine Phosphate (CP):** An organic compound that provides a quick source of energy for muscle fibers to contract when they need an initial burst.

- **Glycogen Depletion:** When carbohydrate levels stored in the liver and muscles converted to glycogen for energy are depleted.

- **Hormonal Variations:** Substances produced by body tissue released within the bloodstream to affect physiological activity, such as growth or metabolism.

- **HR max:** Your maximum heart rate (*MHR*) is the fastest rate at which your heart will beat in one minute.

- **Lactate Threshold (LT):** The lactate threshold is the maximal effort or intensity that an athlete can maintain for an extended period of time with little or no increase in lactate in the blood.

- **Movement Analysis:** The detailed breakdown and analysis of player movement within training.

- **Oxidative Metabolism:** The chemical process in which oxygen is used to make energy from carbohydrates (sugars) to provide energy for working muscles

- **Oxygen Kinetics:** The time it takes for oxygen delivery to respond to the demands of exercise.

- **Oxygen Uptake:** Oxygen consumed by the body during exercise and non-exercise periods.

- **Repeated Sprint Ability (RSA):** The capability of athletes or players to perform short-duration sprints (<10 seconds), interspersed with brief recoveries (<60 seconds).

- **Rate of Perceived Exertion (RPE):** Used to measure the intensity of exercise. Perceived exertion is an individual's rating of exercise intensity, using measurements of heart rate, breathing rate and perspiration/sweating.

- **Running Economy (CR):** The energy demand for a given velocity of sub-maximal running.

- **Stroke Volume (SV):** The volume of blood pumped from the left ventricle of the heart per beat.

- **TDC:** Total distance covered.

- **VO2 max:** The maximum or optimum rate at which the heart, lungs, and muscles can effectively use oxygen during exercise. It is used as a way of measuring a person's individual aerobic capacity (defined below).

- **Work Rate Profiles:** The individual profiles of work performed from a physical and technical perspective.

INTRODUCTION (BOOK SET)

Have you got the other part of this Book Set?

- **FOOTBALL CONDITIONING: A MODERN SCIENTIFIC APPROACH**
  Fitness Training | Speed & Agility | Injury Prevention

Football is considered to be the most popular sport in the world and is played by men, women and children within competitive and non-competitive environments throughout every continent. The 'beautiful game', as many call it, is a multi-million pound industry with huge public and commercial interests that continues to evolve. It has been acknowledged that football performance depends upon a range of factors including technical, tactical, psychological, physical and physiological (Owen et al., 2012; Nedelec et al., 2014; Stølen et al., 2005). It has also been acknowledged that one of the fundamental reasons football is so popular worldwide is due to the fact that players may not need to possess extraordinary levels in each of the performance areas highlighted above, but must require a reasonable capacity across the board (Ingebrigsten et al., 2012; Stølen et al., 2005).

Traditionally, football training has tended to focus primarily on the technical and tactical development of players to the detriment of their physical profile. Recent years have seen a shift towards the use of multi-purpose sessions with the intention of maximising the contact or working time players spend with the technical, physical and medical personnel.

On the basis of recent literature highlighting the use of slightly upgraded and reliable equipment, it may generally be accepted that on average, professional football players cover a distance of 9-12 km during a match (Di Salvo et al., 2006; Barros et al., 2007; Dellal et al., 2011). The first part of this book discusses the movement characteristics (i.e. running distance and intensity) of the game at many levels but focussing on the elite level and how these movement profiles impact the physiological demands imposed.

According to recent literature, elite level football players have good endurance capacities with **VO2 max** (see key terms page) reported to range between 55 and 70 (McMillan et al., 2005; O'Reilly and Wong, 2012) with the game being played at an average intensity close to Lactate Threshold **(LT)** (see key terms page) situated around 80-90% of **HR max** (see key terms page) (Helgerud et al., 2001; McMillan et al., 2005).

Previous research has revealed a link between improvements in players' **aerobic capacity** (see key terms page), increased distance and total number of sprints within competitive games (Helgerud et al., 2001), however further reports are needed to clarify this at the very elite level. According to Dellal et al., (2011) football is predominantly an **'acyclic' sport** (defined as a sport with no set speed, volume or intensity structure – they vary at any given moment based on the opposition and other variables effecting the sport) in which players repeatedly run short distances at a variety of speeds, whilst also covering a substantial distance over the course of a game. It is these short **anaerobic bursts** (see key terms page) that generally decide the outcome of the game (Owen et al., 2012). Strength training within football has recently received more exposure and is suggested to assist from both a performance and injury prevention perspective - see first book in this 2 book set (Campos-Vazquez et al., 2014; Engebretsen et al., 2008; Ekstrand et al., 2011).

The aim of this book set is to make use of the contemporary knowledge within coaching and football science to ultimately further educate individuals working with players of all ages, abilities and levels of play. Increasing the efficiency of the training process and ensuring that key components

of the game (i.e. technical, tactical, physical) are being developed in conjunction with each other, rather than in isolation, is fundamental to the development of this book set. In order to achieve this, the most popular current training methods used on a daily basis within the elite professional game will be discussed. The use of training games (e.g. small, medium and large sided games) within all levels of football is a fundamental training method and is documented as such. However, according to previous research there is relatively little information regarding how these specific functional training games can best be implemented as part of a structured training session in order to collectively improve physical, technical and tactical capacities of football players (Hill-Haas et al., 2011).

Integrating the use of various training games as part of the technical coaching programmes ensures coaches have the opportunity to maximise their contact time with players, increase the efficiency of training and subsequently reduce the total training time due to their multifunctional nature (Dellal et al., 2008; Owen et al., 2004).

Various sided training games have also been suggested to increase player motivation to train when compared to generic running intervals and they create the same effort/work load (Hill-Haas et al., 2009). This book sets out specific justifications for training games and functional practices in order to promote a more efficient training methodology, beneficial for coaches working with a range of playing levels.

Furthermore, setting aside its emergence as a useful training method for aerobic-fitness and technical-tactical development (Hill-Haas et al., 2011), it seems, when compared to actual match play, small sided games may be of insufficient intensity to simulate high-intensity and repeated sprint demands (Casamichana et al., 2012; Gabbett and Mulvey, 2008). These suggestions are reinforced by the reported potential *'ceiling effect'* (limit to the benefits of training) associated with a failure to achieve high exercise intensities in players retaining either high aerobic endurance capacities or technical competency, respectively (Buchheit et al., 2009).

As identified within the literature the need for high intensity and repeated sprint demands is more associated with match play and can potentially be achieved through introducing larger sided games in training (Hill-Hass et al., 2009). These findings may be as a result of large sided games (*LSGs*) being played on bigger pitches, combined with the fact that players in these game formats have less involvement with the ball (Owen et al., 2011). The larger game formats may create different responses as a result of the increased number of sustained high speed/high intensity runs occurring when working 'off the ball' in order to lose opponents or create goal opportunities.

In addition to all of this, the intention of this 2 book set is to draw upon current literature in order to establish the key physical, physiological, technical and tactical demands imposed upon players at the elite professional level of the game. Having outlined and linked these specific demands and in turn highlighted key physical-technical components needed for physical performance development at the elite level, the primary aim of this book set is to further develop the link between contemporary coaching methods and football science principles to maximise the efficiency of training sessions and contact time with players.

Having generated a discussion based upon previous research within the book, attempts to highlight the need for careful preparation, advanced planning, recovery and the successful implementation of a sport specific injury prevention strategy will be proposed (first part of this book set).

CHAPTER 1

FOOTBALL TRAINING AND PRACTICES

FOOTBALL TRAINING AND PRACTICES

1. Periodization in Elite Football

2. The Difference Between 1 or 2 Games per Week

3. Fitness Training in Modern Football

- Pre-Season

- In-Season

- Mid-Season

- Off-Season

4. Specific Training in Elite Modern Football

- Intermittent Exercise

- Speed, Repeated Sprint Ability (*RSA*) and Agility

- Small Sided Games

Throughout recent years the interest and application of more specific training methods attempting to reproduce the technical and physical demands of competitive match play has become more evident (Owen et al., 2011; Owen et al., 2012; Dellal et al., 2010; Koklu et al., 2012). One such method gaining popularity is the use of various sided training games with the aim of applying specific overloads to induce specific outcomes.

Validation for small sided games comes from their ability to develop the technical, tactical and physical abilities of a player at the same time, which in turn helps to enhance training efficiency (Dellal et al., 2012). Many recent studies have shown that by manipulating variables such as technical and tactical constraints (Abrantes et al., 2012), pitch sizes (Casamichana and Castellano, 2010; Kelly and Drust, 2009), player numbers (Hill-Haas et al., 2009) and bout durations (Fanchini et al., (2011), the physiological responses of players can be modified. Favourable physiological responses brought about by this method of training are suggested to fit perfectly within elite level football as a conditioning stimulus capable of improving the *Aerobic Endurance Capacity* - see key terms page (Jones and Drust, 2007; Owen et al., 2011; Coutts et al., 2009; Rampinini et al., 2007; Mallo et al., 2008).

Setting aside its usefulness for training aerobic fitness and technical/tactical development (Hill-Haas et al., 2011), it seems, when compared to actual match play, small sided games may be unable to simulate repeated high speed and sprint demands (Casamichana et al., 2012; Gabbett and Mulvey, 2008). These findings are reinforced by the reported *'Ceiling Effect'* associated with a failure to achieve high exercise intensities (Buchheit et al., 2009).

However, this notion has been disputed by a number of authors working at the elite level (Owen et al., 2012; Dellal et al., 2011). As identified within the literature, high-intensity and repeated sprint demands are more commonly associated with match play when introducing larger sided games formats (Hill-Hass et al., 2009). This may be a result of large sided games (**LSGs**) being played on increased pitch sizes combined with the fact that players in these game formats have less involvement with the ball. This also results in increases of sustained high speed/high intensity runs occurring when working 'off the ball' in order to lose opponents or create a scoring opportunity.

In turn, the lack of research examining medium (6 v 6, 7 v 7, 8 v 8) and larger sided (9 v 9, 10 v 10, 11 v 11) games might be because these games are used more for technical and tactical purposes rather than physiological and physical development. However, not accounting for physical and physiological parameters during these medium and larger sided games may mean that we miss important elements of training and the potential benefits their inclusion may have.

KEY POINT:

It is the authors belief that almost all the technical/tactical drills have a potential physical training effect. The technical and physical development staff should work together to optimise the fitness development within game related training.

The need to generate more football specific training methods and maximise their involvement within a periodized training structure is of paramount importance within the elite level of the game.

Figure 1. An Efficiency Model for the Analysis of Football Training (from Reilly, 2005).

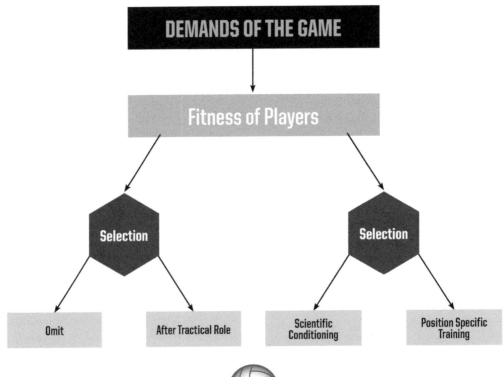

THE TRENDS BETWEEN KEY PERFORMANCE INDICATORS AND LEAGUE POSITION

Figure 2. Trend Association Between Key Performance Indicators and League Position

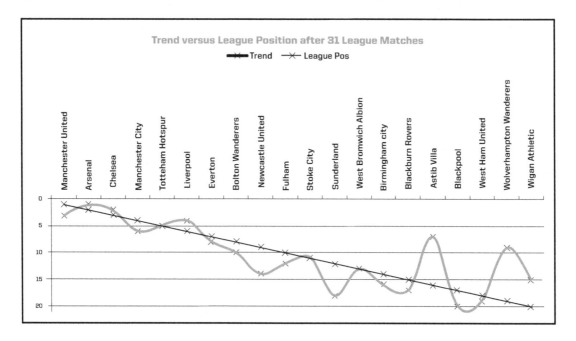

The trend line shows the performance league (produced by PROZONE©) which is based on specific key physical (e.g. total distance covered, sprint distance) and technical (e.g. possession, forward passes) indicators for where the team should be in the league.

The straight line shows the actual league position.

Recent research has shown significant correlations between key football performance indicators (e.g. high-intensity distance covered in/out of possession, sprint distance, successful passes and a team's league ranking (PROZONE©, 2009).

This particular formula has highlighted the key relationship between performance markers and relative success over the season, but further quality research is needed to qualify such suggestions. Previous research detailed later within this chapter has revealed a close relationship between performance testing and team success in elite level Scandinavian football (Arnason et al., 2004; Hoff and Helgerud, 2004).

1. PERIODIZATION IN ELITE FOOTBALL

PERIODIZATION IN ELITE FOOTBALL

What is Periodization?

Training periodization is one of the most utilised theories within numerous individual and team sports throughout the world. The initial concept of 'periodization' was formed in the 1960s and was initially based on the experience of high performance sport in the former USSR, alongside publications from physiologists and scientists working within the Soviet Union sporting family at that current time (Yakovlev, 1955; Zimkin, 1961). Years later the term training periodization was developed, formalised and reproduced throughout many countries and became one of the most allocated theories when planning and analysing training (Matveyev, 1964; Zheliazkov, 1981; Bompa, 1984). According to Issurin, (2010) the continued evolution of sport and sport science has contributed to enhance knowledge, evidence and training technologies, but the traditional model of periodization that was established around 50 years ago has not significantly changed. In recent years, professional reports and coaching magazines have suggested alternative approaches to training design but have been subjected to limited (if any) serious scientific consideration (Issurin, 2010).

The Supercompensation Theory

Supercompensation is a 4 step process. The first step is the application of a training or loading stress and the body's subsequent reaction to this training stress, which is fatigue or tiring. There is a predictable drop-off in performance because of that stress. Step 2 is the recovery phase.

Recent research reported by Issurin (2010) has indicated that in order to understand the basic concept of training periodization, the basic 'load-recovery' interaction or the 'supercompensation theory' must be understood (*Figure 3* on the next page). The supercompensation cycle starts when the player is induced by a physical load, which serves as the stimulus for further reaction. The initial load which

is suggested to be the first phase of the cycle causes an element of fatigue and subsequent limitations of the athlete's work capabilities.

The knock on effect (2nd phase) is then suggested to be characterised by marked fatigue which as a consequence of sufficient recovery, ensures an increase in the athlete's working capability towards the end of this phase, reaching pre-training levels. During the next phase of the sequence, work capability continues to increase, developing ahead of their previous level and achieving the climax, which corresponds to the supercompensation phase (Issurin, 2010).

Furthermore, developing from the earlier reports of the supercompensation theory, it was concluded that a structure involving a number of workouts can be performed in close proximity with the athlete in a fatigued state (Matveyev, 1981). It should be highlighted though, that the supercompensation effect will only be prevalent if the balance between training load and recovery as shown in *Figure 4* (next page), is correct, as this specific effect has been suggested to be positive following a specific small training cycle, but not a single workout. This formation of training cycles set the foundation for the development of small training cycles known as micro-cycles and subsequent pre-competition training development plans.

Figure 3. Supercompensation Cycle - The Trend of Work Capability Following a Single Load (Issurin, 2010).

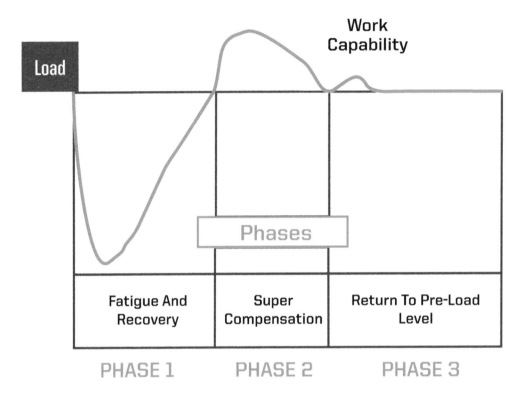

Figure 4. The Link Between Training Load and Recovery Timings (www.pponline.co.uk/encyc/recovery)

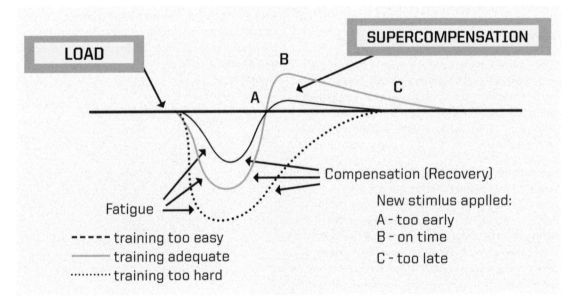

Tapering for Competition

Which framework?

What is tapering?

Tapering is "a progressive reduction of the training load during a variable amount of time that is intended to reduce physiological and psychological stress of daily training and optimise sport performance".

TAPERING STRATEGIES

TRAINING INTENSITY
Should be maintained during taper

TRAINING VOLUME
Maximal gains are obtained with a total reduction of 41-60% of pretaper value

TRAINING FREQUENCY
Decreasing the number of weekly training sessions has not been shown to improve performance

TAPER DURATION
8 to 14 days seems to represent the borderline between fatigue disappearance and the negative influence of detraining

Greater gains in performance can be expected when higher training load is prescribed before the taper. During this period, the focus should be not to develop an overreaching state, which could impair the performance rebound during the taper

INDIVIDUAL RESPONSE

Large individual differences among athletes in the response to tapering are observed. This framework can be useful for coaches to design their training periodization, but it needs to be individualised over time to facilitate peak performance.

Reference: Le Mew, Hausswirth 8 Mujika, Tapering for Competition: A review, Science 8 Sports, 2012

Designed by @YLMSportScience

Training Periodization & Fatigue Management in Football

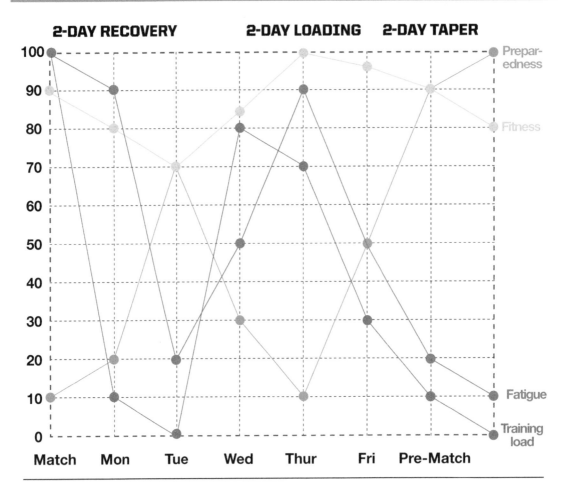

2-DAY RECOVERY   2-DAY LOADING   2-DAY TAPER

Match · Mon · Tue · Wed · Thur · Fri · Pre-Match

Preparedness · Fitness · Fatigue · Training load

Reference

Adopted from Fitness in Soccer - The Science and Practical Applications by Jan Van Winckle et al. 2013

Designed by @YLMSportScience

22

TRAINING CYCLES

Multi-Year Preparation

When discussing a periodized structure in sport, it should be highlighted that this theory is generally part of a multi-year preparation where hierarchical levels are set within the system. As shown in *Table 1* on the next page the top or global system is known as the multi-year preparation, where the aim of attempting to achieve peak performance over a longer term (2-4 year cycles) is of paramount importance (e.g. the Olympics, European Championships, the World Cup).

Macro-Cycles

The next level of the process is known as macro-cycles that are split into months and according to previous research, include preparatory, competition and transition periods (Harre, 1973), generally lasting 1 year, but can be shortened to half a year and even less in some circumstances. There are 3 suggested phases in the macro-cycle:

1) Preparation, 2) Competitive and 3) Transition.

The Preparation Phase

The preparation phase should last approximately 2/3 to 3/4 of the macro-cycle that is broken into 2 parts of equal duration:

- **General Preparation**

  The process of developing an aerobic base for football or endurance related sports.

- **Specific Preparation**

  The process of working on sport specific elements in order to increase efficiency of training.

In some leagues, some teams participate within continental competitions. As a result of these increased fixtures, sometimes players are exposed to extremely short off-season periods. Ideally, football players should take around 3 weeks of rest in between seasons. In that case, the 'preparation phase' can be

quite well structured and start at low intensity to progressively increase the training load. Based on players having a short off-period in between seasons, the preparation (e.g. pre-season) phase should also be significantly shortened. Although there is no science addressing this particular point, the players can resume training after 2 to 3 days of training 'build-up' to ensure an increased training load of high intensity training. It is the opinion of the author, that monitoring training load with adequate tools (RPE, Wellness, HR and GPS analysis) may guide the technical and physical coaching staff to adopt the right training load for each individual player.

The Competitive Phase

The competitive phase can be several competitions or the start of the competitive season in team sport settings. When certain competitions or fixtures are of a higher priority or greater difficulty, then a tapering off stage may be adopted in order to ensure a better physical condition when compared to other competitions or games in the same phase.

The Transition Phase

The last phase is known as the transition phase and is suggested to be important for both physical and psychological reasons. This phase involves a break from training and allows the body and mind to recover fully before the next phase or training cycle.

Meso-Cycles and Micro-Cycles

According to Issurin (2010), the next and shortest period for planning training cycles is mostly used for active recovery and rehabilitation in the training programme and are known as meso-cycles (weeks) and micro-cycles (days). A meso-cycle represents a phase of training over a period of between 2 to 6 weeks but this can depend on the sporting discipline. During the preparatory phase, a meso-cycle commonly consists of 4 to 6 micro-cycles, while during

the competitive phase it will usually consist of 2 to 4 micro-cycles depending on the competitive demands. The long term target is to link the meso-cycles into the overall plan's time line to ensure each meso-cycle ends on one of the phases, as well as ensuring the body peaks for the high priority competitions by improving each cycle along the way.

The smaller meso-cycle and micro-cycle facets are the key foundations of the entire training system. There are few scientific references surrounding the use of periodization in professional football. This may be due to the practical difficulties encountered when trying to implement a long-term periodization strategy within a results based industry. Indeed, the training has to be continuously re-assessed on the fitness evolution of the players, however within professional football

the key is to ensure peak performance is maintained throughout the season as one game across the season is no more important than another from a league campaign. A general plan is possible, but precise training load scheduling has practically no sense on a yearly basis as decreases in physical outputs and performance should not be planned for. The key is to maintain and improve performance markers across the season irrespective of the opposition. It can therefore be suggested that the technical, medical and physical development staff may be more concerned with monitoring and following individual and team trends (e.g. match/training physical, technical loads and outputs) on the basis of micro-cycles or maximally, one meso-cycle.

Table 1. Stages of a Periodized Training Structure – Advanced Planning (Adapted from Issurin, 2010).

TRAINING STAGE	DURATION	TRAINING CONTENT
Multi-Year Preparation	Years	Yearly/multi-year systematic plan developed over 2 or 4 year cycles
Macro-Cycle	Months	Large training cycle includes preparation, competition and transition periods
Meso-Cycle	Weeks	Medium size training cycle consisting of a number of micro-cycles
Micro-Cycle	Days	Small training cycle consisting of a number of days; frequently 1 week
Training Session	Minutes/Hours	A single training session performed individually or within a group

Block Periodization

According to previous research, block periodization has continually been employed with great success in individual sports over many years (Issurin and Kaverin, 1985; Touretski, 1998; Breil et al, 2010). However, research within this area applied to team sport environments is still unclear, (Mallo, 2012) due to the fact that team sports such as football are characterised over very long competition periods with the need to often perform 2 games per week. In one of the only periodization studies within professional football, *author of 'Periodization Fitness Training' Javier Mallo (2011)* investigated the effects of applying a block periodization theory on competitive performance within a professional football team over 4 consecutive competitive seasons. Within the study, the development of different physical capacities relevant for football match performance was organised into consecutive meso-cycles. The training cycles were focussed around 3 training phases, each consisting of the 3 stages of training as proposed by Issurin (2010):

- **The Accumulation Block**

  Mallo (2011) highlighted within the study that the primary aim of *'The Accumulation Block'* was to increase the ability to perform long duration high-intensity intermittent exercise achieved through high-intensity aerobic training.

- **The Transmutation Block**

  'The Transmutation Block' was aimed towards improving players' capacity for repeated sprints with the physical conditioning focus on speed endurance training.

- **The Realisation Block**

  Each training stage concluded with *'The Realisation Block'* to develop players' capacity to perform and reproduce maximum intensity exercise via speed development training.

Based within this training framework, the study examined team success during competition through the assessment of the number of points obtained by the team per match per training stage. Mallo (2011) concluded that the longitudinal study has shown how the physical conditioning of a professional

football team may be structured following a block periodization model due to the highest success percentage in competition being achieved during the realisation blocks, where the team obtained 59% of the points in play. The results of this study show that block periodization may be an alternative training design for professional football teams.

The training of the relevant physical capacities for match performance may be periodized in sequence using specific workloads at the right time in order to allow peak performance at selected stages of the season. The correct appliance workload and recovery bouts may provide the team with the ability to increase the chances of obtaining success at the right time (e.g. advanced planning to ensure the high priority games fall within the realisation stage of training).

Further advances concerning the use of periodization within football have been promoted by recent research concerning this specific training theory (Mallo, 2012). This particular investigation examined the effect of block periodization on physical fitness in a professional football team. Within the study, the competitive season was divided into 5 training stages which were further subdivided into the 3 consecutive blocks as described previously (Accumulation, Transmutation and Realisation). Mallo (2012) highlighted that within this study, the examination of the training volume through the time spent (minutes) developing physical capacities was compared within each block, in conjunction to the heart rate intensity being compared within blocks. Fitness parameters of each player was tested at the end of each training block and compared. Results from the study revealed:

- Time spent performing high-intensity aerobic training was significantly greater in *'The Accumulation Block'* when compared to both the Transmutation and Realisation blocks.

- Time devoted to speed endurance training was higher in *'The Transmutation Block'* when compared to both the Accumulation and Realisation blocks.

- Time spent developing speed was superior in '*The Realisation Block*' when compared to both the Accumulation and Transmutation blocks.

These improvements may be due to the decreased training volume and subsequent supercompensation effect. From a physical performance perspective, it was shown that vertical jump height and 10 metre sprint times improved in the last training stage when compared to the previous 2 phases. Finally, the players covered a 26-30% greater distance in the yo-yo intermittent recovery level 1 test at the end of the season than when compared to the beginning of the competitive period. These results suggest that block periodization can be an alternative design for football training, especially when the key focus is to peak towards the end of the season. This is the key phase of the season when competing for success (trophies), European places or to avoid relegation.

Overall, periodization is suggested to provide a structured framework for planned and systematic variation of training parameters with the primary goal of inducing and maximising sport specific training adaptations (Gamble, 2006; Kelly and Coutts, 2007).

According to recent research, within team sports, typical models of periodization generally follow a logical flow through general preparation, specific preparation, pre-competition, and competition (Dawson, 1996) and although there have been attempts made to apply specific periodization theories to football, additional research is still needed in order to confirm its use in elite level football. Continued research within this area is needed due to the issues surrounding the varying technical, tactical (system of play - in and out of possession) and physical implications. Being able to solely advocate competitive improvement or performance (e.g. points achieved) on a periodized programme brings many difficulties with it, however it certainly opens up the area for further controlled research development.

Figure 5. *Periodization Model of the Football Season* (from Mallo, 2012).

F1			F2			F3		
A	T	R	A	T	R	A	T	R
TS i			TS ii			TS iii		
1	2	3	4	5	6	7	8	9	10	11	12	13	14	15	16	17	18	19	20	21	22	23

F4			F5		
A	T	R	A	T	R
TS iv			TS v		
25	26	27	28	29	30	31	32	33	34	35	36	37	38	39	40	41	42	43	44

*****F** = Fitness Test*; ***A*** = *Accumulation;* ***T*** =*Transmutation;* ***R*** = *Realization;* ***TS*** = *Training Stage*

NOTE: *The last row represents the week number.*

Figure 6. Average Time (Minutes) Spent Per Week in Each Physical Category Within the Training Structure (from Mallo, 2011).

TYPE OF PHYSICAL EXERCISE	ACCUMULATION	TRANSMUTATION	REALISATION
Warm Ups	47.4 ± 8.5	46.1 ± 5.1	47.2 ± 12.3
Low Intensity Aerobic	8.8 ± 22.2	2.0 ± 5.5	0.0 ± 0.0
High Intensity Aerobic	39.2 ± 22.6	6.9 ± 10.5 ***	2.7 ± 6.6 ***
Gym Based Strength	36.5 ± 23.4	16.2 ± 11.1 *	13.7 ± 10.3 **
Speed Endurance	2.8 ± 4.0 sss	21.0 ± 10.1	9.3 ± 12.4 s
Speed	9.3 ± 6.5 #	10.5 ± 10.4 *	21.1 ± 12.4
Flexibility	29.0 ± 14.6	22.5 ± 7.6	21.4 ± 2.4
Other Capacities	3.7 ± 4.5	6.6 ± 5.0	6.5 ± 6.7

* Significant difference from Accumulation (P <0.05)   *=$ Significant difference from Transmutation (P <0.05)*
** Significant difference from Accumulation (P <0.01)   *$ $ Significant difference from Transmutation (P <0.001)*
*** Significant difference from Accumulation (P <0.001)   *# Significant difference from Realisation (P <0.05)*

Figure 7. Percentage of Points Won in Relation to Total Points Available in the Accumulation, Transmutation and Realisation Meso-Cycles When playing Against Teams from the Spanish 3rd Division (from Mallo, 2011).

Top = Top teams in positions 1st-6th; Middle = Middle teams in positions 7th-13th; Bottom = Bottom teams in positions 14th-20th

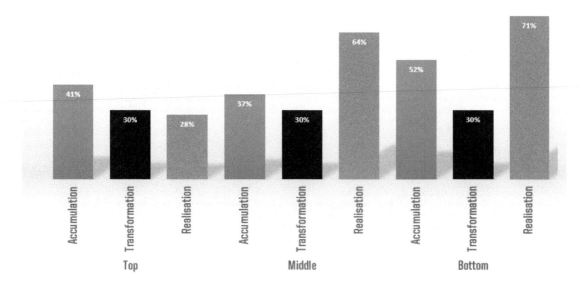

POINTS OBTAINED (%)

PERIODIZATION PARADIGMS IN THE 21st CENTURY: EVIDENCE LED OR TRADITION DRIVEN?

By John Kiely, International Journal of Sport Physiology and Performance, 2012

OBSERVATIONS

1 Individual athletes will respond differently to identical training sessions

2 Identical sessions performed by an individual will always elicit a unique training response for that athlete, depending on transient functional states of component subsystems

3 Group-based patterns and observations may be highly misleading when generalised to individuals

4 It is highly improbable that there are "best" patterns, time frames, or progressions and/or loading schemes applicable across all training contexts

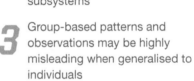

Such reasoning suggests a shift from the historical ideal of preordained "best" training structures toward a philosophy characterised by an adaptive readiness to respond to emerging "information"

PRACTICAL IMPLICATIONS

1 Deviation from the preplanned path is desirable, should be actively sought, and the training management system should be designed to facilitate, rather than suppress consistent modulation.

2 A crucial component of effective training processes is the systematic capture and review of pertinent data that are then employed to drive future direction.

Designed by @YLMSportScience

Football Conditioning: A Modern Scientific Approach

Training Load and Tapering Strategies

- The integrated use of technology to monitor training, from both external and internal loading perspectives have increased, however, the underlying focus toward respectively quantifying training drills and game format types which best stimulate the technical, tactical and physical demands of match play has gained recent interest to practitioners. Overall, in general the implementation and efficacy of periodization practices within an elite football setting remains currently poorly understood and reported.

- One recent research study by Malone et al. (2014) quantified the seasonal training load in an elite English Premier League squad and observed periodization of training load was typically confined to the day preceding a competitive match (MD-1), whereas no differences were apparent during MD-2 to MD-5.

- Furthermore, Owen et al., (2016 unpublished) provided an in-season analysis of a training mesocycle and quantification of micro-cycle positional demands in elite European football players whilst describing a specific tapering method used in preparation towards competitive match play. Results revealed that using this specific tapering model, practitioners could maintain a uniformed and structured meso-cycle whilst inducing a significant variation in the training load outputs during the micro-cycle period. Subsequently, this tapering strategy enhanced the potential to impose significantly reduced physical stressors upon players within a 48hr period preceding the competitive match whilst reducing an accumulative fatigue response.

- Additionally, the investigation also revealed how this tapering approach may induce significant variations within positional demands throughout a micro-cycle, and further stress the importance of training players as individuals in relation to their positional training loads.

- Coaches need to ensure they acknowledge tapering strategies exist within elite level football, and as a result, place an overloaded stimulus within the micro-cycle in order to maximise performance and reduce fatigue close to match day.

2. THE DIFFERENCE BETWEEN 1 OR 2 GAMES A WEEK

THE DIFFERENCE BETWEEN 1 OR 2 GAMES A WEEK

Current elite professional football requires players to possess the ability to recover from competitive matches and high intensity training periods. This suggested link between players being able to compete continually at these high intensity and high speed levels, as well as being able to recover to sufficient levels is considered to be a determining factor in subsequent performance (Mohr et al, 2005).

The physical, technical and psychological demands imposed upon players throughout the course of the season are generally dependent upon the success of teams (e.g. increased number of games associated with being successful: Champions League; UEFA Cup; domestic cup competitions), as well as individual success (e.g. players being selected for international competition: World Cups; European Championships etc) as shown in *Table 2* below. On the back of these suggestions, elite professional football players are often required to play competition matches every 3 to 4 days, with only 2 to 3 days' recovery between fixtures.

Table 2. Number of Official Matches Played Within Elite European Leagues (from Dellal et al., 2013).

COUNTRY	NUMBER OF LEAGUE MATCHES	NUMBER OF LEAGUE CUP MATCHES	NUMBER OF NATIONAL CUP MATCHES	NUMBER OF CHAMPIONS LEAGUE MATCHES	OTHER CLUB MATCHES	NATIONAL TEAM MATCHES	MINIMUM AMOUNT OF GAMES	MAXIMUM AMOUNT OF GAMES	SUMMER HOLIDAYS (DAYS)
Spain (La Liga)	38	1 to 10	0	6 to 15	2 to 4	4 to 11	51	78	30 to 41
England (Premier League)	38	1 to 9	1 to 9	6 to 15	2	4 to 11	52	84	40 to 55
Germany (Bundesliga)	34	1 to 5	1 to 6	6 to 15	1	4 to 11	47	72	41 to 53
France (Ligue 1)	38	1 to 5	1 to 6	6 to 15	2	4 to 11	50	77	25 to 35
Italy (Serie A)	38	2 to 11	0	6 to 15	1	4 to 11	51	76	41 to 53

PHYSICAL PREPARATION DURING CONGESTED FIXTURE PERIODS

Under such aggressive and congested fixture periods, the maintenance or improvement of players' physical capabilities may not only be determined by the pre-competitive conditioning level but also by a player's ability to structurally, biochemically and psychologically recover and regenerate after multiple loadings (e.g. matches; training sessions) (Ekstrand et al, 2011; Hagglund et al, 2005).

Recent research studied the physical activity profiles and injury rates of professional football players during intense periods of matches (Carling et al, 2012; Carling and Dupont, 2011). Interestingly, results from the investigation did not reveal any differences in the distances covered at various speeds and the injury risk across successive matches played within a congested fixture period. Within this research area, the key findings from numerous authors have revealed how high-intensity running (*HIR*) and the injury rate of the players remained unaffected with minimal recovery days between fixtures (Carling et al, 2010; Carling et al, 2012).

It should be noted however, that these specific findings should be taken with care due to specific limitations of the studies:

1. The number of players studied varied from match to match.

2. Only 6 players took part in every game as starters or substitutes

3. Only 1 outfield player completed every game studied.

Due to these limitations, further extensive research is needed in order to investigate the effects of congested fixture periods and short between-game recovery bouts on the physical activity and injury rates of elite professional players.

Additionally, one of the most substantial investigations examining the differences between playing 1 or 2 matches per week has been performed by Dupont and colleagues (2010). The study concentrated on the recovery time between 2 competitive matches played within a 7 day period. It was concluded that:

1. A 72 to 96 hour recovery period between games appeared to be sufficient in order to maintain levels of physical performance in the consecutive games (i.e. no significant reductions in high-intensity and sprint distance covered).

2. However, this period of time between games was reported as insufficient when trying to maintain reduced injury rates.

3. Subsequently, from a practical perspective, the findings of the study propose the need for larger squads, player rotation, injury prevention techniques and improved recovery strategies with the primary aim of maintaining a reduced injury rate during periods with congested match fixtures is essential.

The Effects of Intensity, Volume and Training Load

To date there seems to be a limited amount of research investigating the effects of intensity, volume and loadings when comparing the difference between 1 and 2 fixtures per week. One of the limited publications surrounding this area compared 1 versus 2 fixtures per week amongst English professional players over a 20 week period during the competitive season (Owen and Wong, 2009). Results from the study revealed that the weekly high-intensity volume was reduced by 27% and 67% respectively for weeks with 1 or 2 matches, compared with those weeks that had no match (*Table 3* on next page).

KEY POINT:

Larger squads, player rotation, injury prevention techniques and improved recovery strategies with the primary aim of maintaining a reduced injury rate during periods with congested match fixtures is essential.

Table 3. Volume of High-Intensity (HI) Training Based on Weekly Number of Matches
(from Owen and Wong, 2009)

NUMBER OF GAMES PER WEEK	REDUCTION IN HI TRAINING IN COMPARISION TO 0 GAMES PER WEEK (%)	VOLUME OF HI INTENSITY TRAINING PER WEEK	
		Average	S.D (±)
0 games per week	–	55.57	6.14
1 game per week	25.70	41.29	9.55
2 games per week	67.30	18.17	8.29

*** High Intensity (HI) Training** = Time (mins) >85%HRmax*

Likewise, Impellizzeri et al (2005) reported that training weeks including 2 official matches within an Italian professional football team may see on average a 50% reduction of total weekly training load as shown in *Figure 8 (A)* on the next page. Furthermore, it was suggested that when one match per week is played, the total training load reduction is only 25% as shown in *Figure 9 (B)*, which are very similar to those findings proposed by Owen and Wong (2009). Due to the conclusions of the previous research, it is of paramount importance that the formulation and validation of methods are developed in order to quantify the aerobic cost and internal training load in competitive football matches and to further understand the physical load, training effects and recovery procedures aimed at maximising players' physical capacity.

Planning Training for Substitutes and Unused Players

One major issue linked with having the team playing 2 games in a week is finding the right balance of training for starters, squad and non-squad players. It is clear that when playing 2 games a week, the training load of first team players during training sessions decreases (as pointed out here above). The coaching staff should look to manage the players who are not taking part in the games or have only been involved as substitutes differently. The capacity to precisely monitor the different playing status' will greatly determine the efficiency of the coaching staff.

Ensuring the non-playing squad and substitutes competitive match minutes lost are replaced in the correct manner and at the right time (e.g. reserve games, high speed and high intensity training) is of huge importance as these players become important players across the season.

Reductions in the physical capacities of these players can have negative effects when they are called upon to replace the regular starting players. From a practical application perspective, technical and physical staff unable to establish such strategies, will notably end up with players of 2 different status' within the squad:

1. The starting or regular players who are physically prepared through regular training and competitive matches.

2. The regular substitutes or non-playing squad members who over time, progressively lose their physical capacity and psychological focus as they enter into a "detrained state".

KEY POINT:

Ensuring the non-playing squad and substitutes competitive match minutes lost are replaced in the correct manner and at the right time (e.g. reserve games, high speed and high intensity training) is of huge importance as these players become important players across the season.

Figures 8-9. Weekly Periodization (1 vs. 2 Games Per Week) in an Italian Professional Football Team
(from Impellizzeri et al, 2005).

RPE-TLd = *Rate of Perceived Exertion - Training Load (RPE x Training Duration)*

Figure 8. Two Games Per Week (A)
* Match days in grey, **training days in blue**

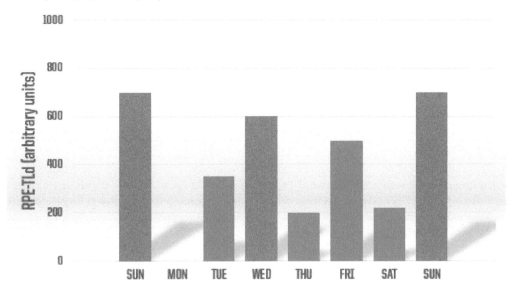

Figure 9. One Game Per Week (B)
* Match days in grey, **training days in blue**

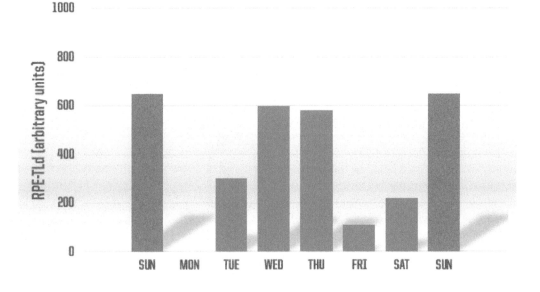

FOOTBALL
Effects of an intensive fixture schedule

No effect
on technical
performance

Decreased
Immune
Function

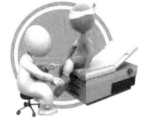

Possible but not systematic
decrease in Stress Recovery Index

Possible but not
systematic
decrease
in physical
performance

**High importance of squad rotation
& post-match recovery strategies**

Possible but not systematic
increase in muscle injuries rates

REFERENCE
Dupont et al. Int J Sports Med, 38(9), 2010
Carling et al. Int J Sports Med, 33(1), 2012
Bengtsson et al. Br J Sports Med, 47(12), 2013
Dellal et al. Br J Sports Med, 2013
Rollo et al. Int J Sports Physiol Perform, 9(3), 2014
Morgans et al. Res Sports Med, 2014
McCormack et al. Int J Sports Physiol Perform, 2014

Designed by @YLMSportScience

CONGESTED FIXTURE PERIODS: TACTICAL & PHYSICAL PERFORMANCE *in elite football*

By Fogaldo et al., JSS 2015

6 HOME MATCHES
of an English Professional Football Team During a Competitive Season

PREMIER LEAGUE
3 matches
≥ 6 DAYS
from the previous fixture

3 matches
3 DAYS
from the previous fixture

PHYSICAL PERFORMANCES
Measured by the total distance covered and distance covered in different speed categories

TACTICAL PERFORMANCES
Measured by the percentage of time players' movement was synchronised (lateral & longitudinal displacements)

Results

1 No differences in the physical performance, although players spent more time synchronised during the non-congested fixtures compared to congested fixtures

2 These coordination differences were particularly evident at the lower speed categories and in pairs composed by positions that tend to be further apart during the match, typically central and wing positioned players

Potential Implications

This data constitutes an interesting point for coaches, as players may need specific recovery interventions for dealing with match demands beyond individual physical recovery. For instance, players groups who presented a lower synchronisation level during congested fixtures might benefit from:

Specific positioning and group coordination training sessions, complementary or interrelated physical recovery

Designed by @YLMSportScience

3. FITNESS TRAINING IN MODERN FOOTBALL

FITNESS TRAINING IN MODERN FOOTBALL

How can managers and coaching staff play a specific system or style of play if the players are physically incapable to cope with the positional demands?

The development and maintenance of key physical fitness components throughout the course of the season is paramount for every team irrespective of the level of competition (Koutedakis, 1995). The development of players' physical profiles and subsequent fitness levels is a very complex process due to the diversity in the physical demands of the game, with respect to their positional differences.

There are many different facets to competing at the elite level and ensuring technical, tactical, psychological, physical and physiological components are being enhanced and maintained through the various stages of the season (e.g. pre-season, in-season, end of season) is fundamental to the

performance and subsequent success of the team. Contemporary literature has reported how more functional fitness training sessions (e.g. intermittent aerobic work, position specific practices, various sided games) are becoming more popular at the elite level due to their efficiency and the fact that they can influence technical, tactical and physical components all at once, as opposed to being developed in isolation (Hill-Haas et al, 2011; Owen et al, 2011; Owen et al, 2012; Dellal et al, 2011; Dellal et al, 2012). According to Kelly and Coutts (2007), coaches are continually faced with issues regarding the application of appropriate training loads during the competition phase of the season and ensuring these loads are met without negating any other component.

Figure 10. Diagram to Show the Key Component Interactions

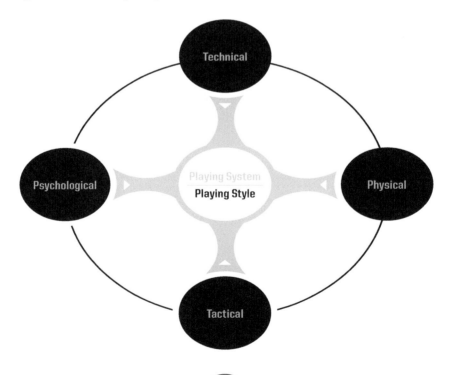

PRE-SEASON

The evaluation of training programmes in football is vital in order to establish the strengths, weaknesses and subsequent effectiveness of methods used. The pre-season phase of football training gives technical and physical coaches the opportunity to implement a periodized structure with the primary aim of increasing physical, technical and tactical aspects of the players under a controlled process.

From the pre-season phase onwards, the opportunity to continually improve elements of match-play is performed under a slightly less controlled process, due to the continual demands placed upon the coaching staff and players during domestic, European and international fixtures, combined with the additional travelling and logistical issues surrounding these.

Testing players' key physical variables before the start and towards the end of pre-season is a process which will allow coaches of all interests to expose weaknesses and subsequently attempt to improve them through specific training.

Throughout the pre-season preparation period, the training focus is placed upon ensuring the key sport specific muscle groups and energy systems are being stimulated in order to cause positive adaptations, leading to improvements in aerobic endurance, strength, speed and power (Dellal, 2008). Pre-season itself generally follows a process of developing general fitness, then specific fitness, before moving into the pre-competition preparation phase (*Figure 11* below).

KEY POINT:

Throughout pre-season, the training focus is placed upon ensuring the key sport specific muscle groups and energy systems are being stimulated in order to cause positive adaptations, leading to improvements in aerobic endurance, strength, speed and power.

Figure 11. Development of Training Load (Volume and Intensity) Throughout the Pre-Season Phase

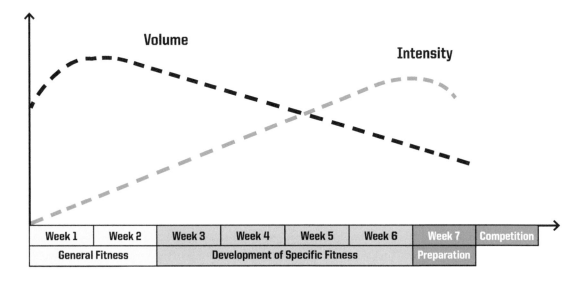

The concurrent nature of training for both strength and high-intensity aerobic adaptations has long caused controversy within the literature, with previous authors questioning the potential to improve more than one key football fitness component at the same time, within a limited period (Dudley and Djamil, 1985; Bishop et al, 1999; Sale et al, 1990). Furthermore, previous research has suggested that high-intensity endurance training may inhibit or interfere with the strength developments trying to be achieved if trained at the same time (Chromiac and Mulvaney, 1990; Hennessy and Watson,1994).

Additionally, previous research examining the physiological effects of concurrent strength and aerobic training, has suggested that there has been no systematic approach to what is known as the 'interference phenomenon' between these two modes of training (Docherty and Sporer, 2000). This is suggested to be due to the fact that individual laboratories focus their research on one particular training model or method and subsequently perform series of investigations surrounding their model or mode of training (Leveritt et al, 1999). Due to the physiological adaptations resulting from the different training protocols aimed at developing aerobic power and strength, Docherty and Sporer (2000) proposed a model that may assist in providing a way to scientifically examine the 'interference phenomenon' further. Docherty and Sporer (2000) developed the model shown below (*Figure 12*) in order to allow the development of hypotheses that may predict which training protocols carry a higher or lower risk of interference while simultaneously training for strength and aerobic developments. Furthermore, it was also suggested that this model may lead to the potential of constructing similar theories enabling the systematic development of interference effects between different fitness components.

Figure 12. The Training Interference Phenomenon (adapted from Docherty and Sporer, 2000).

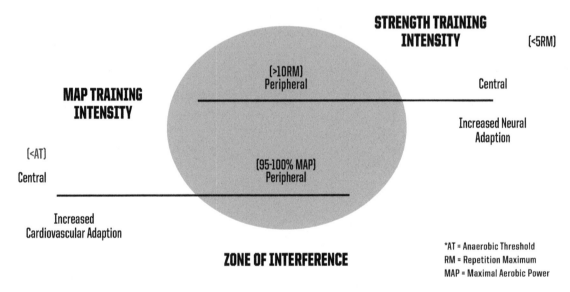

The model above (*Figure 12*), proposed for the investigation of concurrent strength and aerobic training, has focused primarily on the manipulation of training intensity, with suggestions of there being an inverse relationship between intensity and volume of training. According to Docherty and Sporer (2000), normally as the training intensity (lifting load - kg) and aerobic intensity (*%VO2max*) increases, the volume (duration, sets x repetitions) would decrease. Using the model, it would be hypothesised that interference would be maximised when athletes use high-intensity interval training to improve aerobic power and a

large volume resistance training protocol to increase strength.

Recent research positively confirming the effects of concurrent muscular strength and high-intensity intervals throughout the pre-season phase have been reported. Wong et al, (2010) concluded that:

- During the pre-season period, concurrent muscular strength and high-intensity interval running training can be used in order to enhance professional football players' explosive performance in conjunction to their intermittent and continuous aerobic endurance.

- In order to minimise the 'interference phenomenon' (described previously) when using concurrent strength and aerobic training modes, high load and less repetition are recommended in muscular strength training (6 reps for 4 sets, with 3 minutes of rest between sets).

- Likewise, high-intensity interval running e.g. 15 seconds at 120% of maximal aerobic speed (*MAS*) with passive recovery could be used to effectively improve aerobic endurance (Dellal et al, 2010).

Besides the positive pre-season work of Wong et al, (2010), both Hoff and Helgerud (2002) and Vieira et al, (2012) revealed how following a structured programme with 60-85% of normal strength training loads showed improvements in explosive strength (squat jumps), 10 metre sprint times and other tests during pre-season.

When discussing the increasing levels of aerobic endurance performance over the pre-season phase, McMillan et al (2005) had recently shown how dribbling a football around a specially designed track as part of high intensity aerobic interval training (4 x 4 minutes at 90-95% *HRmax*) among professional football players can elevate *VO2max* levels from low, to moderate values, to that of elite Champions League football players, with no negative interference effects on strength, jumping ability, and sprint performance.

Although the research by McMillan et al (2005), Helgerud et al (2001) revealed improved aerobic

capacity with no negative implications to speed and power development, the nature of the 'football specific' intervention should be questioned. According to recent literature, coaches now tend to focus the overload of training by manipulating the player numbers involved within *SSGs* (3 v 3; 4 v 4) as suggested by Owen et al (2011). According to Dellal et al (2011) this adds greater motivation, sport specific movements and energy systems recruited.

Overall, pre-season for many professional football clubs is vitally important to the longer sustainability of players' match and training availability throughout the duration of the season. Research findings suggest that if sport science, technical and medical staff do not implement a periodized structure, gradually increasing the physical fitness of players, then more injuries may be sustained throughout the pre-season phase due to the training overload - Owen et al (2013) revealed that most muscle injuries occur within the pre-season phase of the season. This may be attributed to the increased training load or lack of periodization in the planning phase. To date, the authors are not aware of any literature to support the notion that players who do not fulfill the majority of the pre-season period may have a higher risk of injury during the in-season period, however as proposed, further research is needed in this area to confirm this statement.

KEY POINTS:

1. *During the pre-season period, concurrent muscular strength and high-intensity interval running training can be used in order to enhance professional football players' explosive performance in conjunction to their intermittent and continuous aerobic endurance.*

2. *If sport science, technical and medical staff do not implement a periodized structure, gradually increasing the physical fitness of players, then more injuries may be sustained throughout the pre-season phase due to the training overload.*

INTERFERENCE BETWEEN RESISTANCE AND ENDURANCE EXERCISE:
THE ROLE OF TRAINING VARIABLES

By Jackson J. Fyfe • David J. Bishop • Nigel K. - Stepto *Sports Medicine, 2014*

Concurrent training is defined as simultaneously incorporating both resistance and endurance exercise within a periodized training regime. Despite the potential additive benefits of combining these divergent exercise modes, current evidence suggests that this approach may create gains in muscle mass, strength, and power compared with undertaking resistance training alone.

Specific concurrent training variables might make molecular interference worse, either indirectly by compromising the 'quality' of the resistance exercise itself or directly by increasing the activity of proteins acting to inhibit protein synthesis and/or stimulate protein breakdown. Improving your knowledge of the contribution of these variables to the interference effect is therefore critical to learn how to best maximise the simultaneous development of muscle mass, strength and endurance.

1 WITHIN SESSION EXERCISE ORDER

Performing aerobic exercise in close proximity to resistance exercise decreases anabolic signaling and increases catabolic activity, which likely represents acute interference of pathways governing resistance training. It is recommended that both exercise modes be performed with significant recovery periods to minimise acute interference, and that resistance training precede repeated sprints if performed within the same session.

2 PROXIMITY

Divergent exercise modes can be successfully performed on the same day without compromising performance or the molecular responses mediating protein synthesis and mitochondrial biogenesis. However, whether shorter recovery lengths would have made any putative molecular interference worse is unclear.

3 ENDURANCE TRAINING INTENSITY

High-intensity endurance exercise may increase acute molecular interference when compared with lower-intensity endurance exercise. Higher intensity endurance exercise also appears to inhibit subsequent force production, whilst low-intensity continuous exercise may cause less residual fatigue. Finally, higher exercise intensities are associated with increased glycogen depletion occurring predominantly in type II muscle fibers, which may notably increase the chances of residual fatigue.

4 ENDURANCE TRAINING VOLUME

It remains to be determined whether the total weekly endurance training volume, or the training frequency is the more critical factor of concurrent interference. If endurance exercise volume is key, low-volume **High-intensity Intermittent Training (HIT)** protocols might be benefitial when incorporating concurrent training by limiting any potential volume-dependent interference effect, whilst also offering similar metabolic and performance benefits to traditional endurance exercise.

5 ENDURANCE TRAINING MODE

The majority of concurrent training studies reporting an interference effect have incorporated running, and less often cycling. Relatively little is known regarding the impact of running exercise on acute post-exercise adaptive responses in skeletal muscle, compared with cycling or swimming.

Designed by @YLMSportScience

JUST HOW IMPORTANT IS A GOOD SEASON START?

By Lago-Peñasa & Jaime Sampaio, J Sports Sci, April 2015

Match performances and annual budgets from the English FA Premier League, French Ligue 1, Spanish La Liga, Italian Serie A and German Bundesliga clubs were collected

The better the team performance at the beginning of the season, the better the ranking at the end of the season

3 consecutive seasons analysed
FROM 2010-2011 TO 2012-2013

A greater importance of having a good season start was reported for the clubs with lower budgets

WHAT DOES IT SUGGEST?

Clubs with lower-mid and low range budgets can particularly benefit from fine-tuning pre-season planning in order to accelerate the process of achieving optimal performances

Designed by @YLMSportScience

IN-SEASON

In order to develop fitness components and remain at peak fitness throughout the course of the season, it requires the combination of fitness, technical and medical staff working as a close cohesive unit. This approach ensures the training data may be analysed and monitored in order to provide the correct stimulus intensity to improve physical qualities, reducing the risk of overload and fatigue related injuries at the same time. Within the literature surrounding elite level professional football, training intensity and load has been monitored and reported in many different ways. It is now common for top level professional football teams to monitor training load using various pieces of technical equipment such as heart rate monitors (Owen et al, 2011; Bangsbo et al, 2006) and global positioning systems (GPS) (Koklu et al, 2012; Owen et al, 2013). The *HR* and *GPS* systems provide important information regarding the external (i.e. distance, speed) and internal (i.e. heart rate) training demands imposed upon players. In addition to the technical devices used to provide information

regarding training intensity and loads, both previous and recent research has championed the use of ratings of perceived exertion *(RPE)* as an alternative, valid and time effective method for calculating training intensity during an entire football training session composed of small sided games, speed, tactical, technical, conditioning and plyometric training (Coutts et al, 2009; Impellizzeri et al., 2004).

Specifically at the elite level of professional football, key issues such as opposition quality, number of training days between matches, as well as any travelling associated with the fulfilment of fixtures, influence the weekly or monthly training intensity. Understanding these factors as a combination may assist as a guide when planning the weekly or monthly training activity. Kelly and Coutts (2007) have proposed a model for team sports that may be able to help coaches assist in development of the correct training load by predicting the loading of specific competitive games (*Figure 13* below).

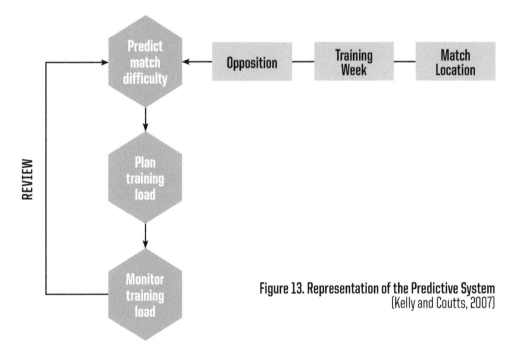

Figure 13. Representation of the Predictive System (Kelly and Coutts, 2007)

In a similar but novel approach, research by Cormack (2001) suggested a working advanced planning model for an Australian Rules Football League team. The model focussed itself on the number of training days between matches in accordance to the effects caused by travel. This particular investigation revealed how micro-cycles may be manipulated in order to maximise recovery in conjunction to the development of technical and tactical components (Cormack, 2001). The success of an in-season plan is suggested to be affected by various components such as the understanding of the training process by the technical staff involved, in accordance with the training, rest, recovery balance and the monitoring and application of training load and volume. According to Cormack, (2001) this suggested a tendency with technical staff to react to the situation, result of a game, or use intuition, rather than follow a specific plan.

Kelly and Coutts (2007) proposed through their model, that when they are preparing for a difficult match (e.g. strong opposition, limited preparation time, long duration away travel), it may be sensible to plan a lighter training week with a reduction of training load to minimise the potential of accumulative fatigue. On the contrary, sufficient recovery between games combined with a home fixture against a potentially suggested weaker opponent, may provide an opportunity to increase the training load to positively influence the conditioning levels of the playing squad. Performed in a football specific way, the development of technical, physical and tactical components may be enhanced in a more efficient and productive way.

The coaching staff will have to find the right balance between decreasing *Training Load (TL)* to avoid fatigue/stress, and increasing it to keep the training improvements. This will have to be done with a range of training loads. For instance, professional football players from Tunisia over several seasons have shown that decreasing the *TL* or increasing it had potential detraining/overtraining effects, respectively. Each player has to be considered individually and the coaching staff has to find the right balance of *TL* in order to manage everyone's fitness, while avoiding detraining/overreaching.

Rate of Perceived Exertion (RPE)

With the system proposed by Kelly and Coutts (2007) - *Figure 13* on the previous page, players are required to provide a *Rate of Perceived Exertion (RPE)* from 1-10, with 1 being easy and 10 being very difficult for each exercise that is then multiplied by the training session duration (minutes) to determine training load. The simplicity of this system makes it effective for quantifying training load in team sports.

The focus of Kelly and Coutts (2007) model was to outline a simplistic model that can be used to predict match difficulty in team sport and link through an *RPE* system in order to guide the training process in team sports. When developing an in-season (i.e. competition phase) training programme it is important to have a simple system that allows the coach to predict the difficulty of each match, plan the weekly training load accordingly, and review the programme on a regular basis.

KEY POINTS:

1. *Opposition quality, number of training days between matches, as well as any travelling associated with the fulfilment of fixtures, should influence the weekly or monthly training intensity. Understanding these factors as a combination may assist as a guide when planning the weekly or monthly training activity.*

2. *When developing an in-season (i.e. competition phase) training programme it is important to have a simple system that allows the coach to predict the difficulty of each match, plan the weekly training load accordingly, and review the programme on a regular basis.*

In-Season Anaerobic and Aerobic Fitness

The previous section discussed how the pre-season training phase tends to focus around the development of many different physical fitness components with and without the ball. During the in-season period, the emphasis is primarily concentrated on making tactical/technical improvements and ensuring physical fitness is maintained (Dupont et al, 2004). It has been suggested that because competitive match-play requires higher energy expenditure, the weekly training load is maintained in order to avoid excessive fatigue or the beginning of an overtraining syndrome (Dupont et al, 2004). Recent studies have claimed aerobic fitness improves among players throughout the course of the season (Haritonidis et al, 2004; McMillan et al, 2002; Metaxas et al, 2006). In this context, McMillan et al (2005) also reported that players showed lower lactate concentration at fixed running velocities throughout the season, suggesting an improvement in fitness levels. In such cases, when using a heart rate based monitoring tool, players may have a lower heart rate for the same exercise intensity later in the season, compared with early in the season.

Contemporary interventions inclusive of both football specific and non-football specific training performed during the in-season period, have revealed positive effects on both the anaerobic and aerobic systems. Previous in-season studies have reported significant improvements in *VO2max* (Hoff and Helgerud, 2004; McMillan et al., 2005) and maximal aerobic speed (*MAS*) (Dupont et al., 2004) through the use of high-intensity non-football specific interventions. Furthermore, the integration of an in-season periodized small sided game intervention led to a significant improvement in *RSA* (i.e. reduced sprint times, total sprint time, and % reduction scores) as shown in *Table 4* below (Owen et al., 2012). There were also running economy improvements shown through reduced oxygen uptake and heart rate values. Findings from the study conclude that football specific sessions can be used as an alternative to traditional training methods to improve physical fitness in-season at the elite level. To the author's knowledge, the study by Owen et al., (2012) is the only published journal to reveal the impact of a small sided game training intervention on elite players' physical performance.

Table 4. The Effects of SSGs Training Intervention on Players' Physical Performance (from Owen et al., 2012).

RSA	PRE-SSG	POST-SSG
10m FST	1.77	1.75
20m FST	3.08	3.06
TST	18.96	18.61
% Reduction	2.43%	1.48%

RSA = *Repeated Sprint Ability*
PRE-SSG = *Data before the players take part in a small sided game*
POST-SSG = *Data after the players take part in a small sided game*
FST = *Fastest Sprint Time (seconds)*
TST = *Total Sprint Time (seconds)*

MID-SEASON

It seems that many professional football clubs implement physiological testing structures throughout the course of the season (generally pre-season, mid-season and end of season), therefore allowing physiological trends to be highlighted.

Published work in this area tends to highlight the effects of different applied training methods on the aerobic capacity, speed, power and speed endurance of football players across the season (McMillan et al, 2005; Ostojic, 2003; Clark et al, 2008; Jastrzebsk et al, 2011). Findings from such investigations reveal contrasting opinions concerning players' physical state depending upon when training interventions have been implemented.

Jastrzebsk et al, (2011) reported how 1st team players with the highest match availability and game time across the season posted the highest levels of aerobic fitness (*VO2max*) in the middle of the season, while substitute players with less playing time scored highest at the end of the season. When comparing this data set against previous studies inclusive of both football and non-football specific in-season high-intensity interventions, conflicting reports are prevalent from a physiological perspective (Owen et al, 2012; McMillan et al, 2005; Hoff et al, 2004; Dupont et al, 2004). These conflicting values are probably due to the different methodologies and subject groups that were used in each case.

Recent research by Owen and Wong (2009) revealed how, as an English professional team's season progressed from pre-season through to the mid-phase of the season, the monthly high-intensity training volume decreased (*Table 5* on the next page).

Previous studies have showed how the *Total Distance Covered (TDC), High-Intensity Distance Covered (HIDC)* and the sprint distance of top level players during matches increased throughout the competitive season (Mohr et al, 2003; Rampinini et al, 2007). Therefore, it may be reasonable to suggest that the

reduction in volume of high-intensity training through the mid-season phase links to the long term plan, ensuring maximal fitness and freshness by avoiding any accumulative fatigue-induced injuries in the preparation of competitive fixtures.

Other potential explanations for the decreased volume of high intensity training is due to more time being spent on technical and tactical components rather than the continued development of fitness levels, however further research is needed to justify this proposal.

KEY POINTS:

1. *1st team players with the highest match availability and game time across the season posted the highest levels of aerobic fitness (VO2max) in the middle of the season, while substitute players with less playing time scored highest at the end of the season.*

2. *The Total Distance Covered (TDC), High-Intensity Distance Covered (HIDC) and the sprint distance of top level players during matches increased throughout the competitive season.*

3. *The reduction in volume of training while maintaining the intensity of training through the mid to end of season phase ensures key progression of fitness and freshness through avoidance of accumulative fatigue-induced injuries.*

Table 5. *Monthly Volume of High-Intensity Training* (>85%HRmax) *Shown Through Number of Minutes Per Day* (from Owen and Wong, 2009).

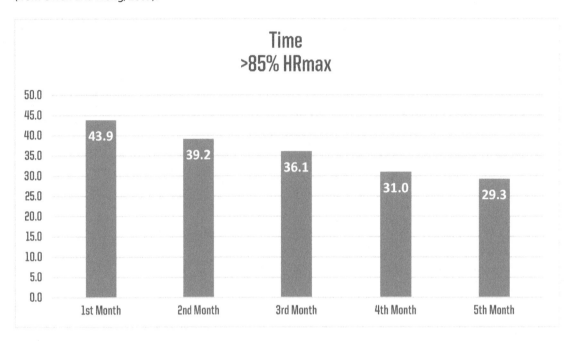

EFFECT OF SHORT TERM INTERVAL TRAINING DURING THE COMPETITIVE SEASON ON PHYSICAL FITNESS AND SIGNS OF FATIGUE IN HIGH LEVEL YOUTH FOOTBALL PLAYERS

By O. Faude, A. Steffen, M. Kellmann & T. Meyer, IJSPP, November 2014

The aim of this study was to analyse performance and fatigue effects of Small Sided Games (SSGs) vs. High-Intensity Interval Training (HIIT) performed during a 4 week in-season period within high level youth football

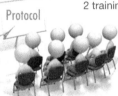

WHAT DID THEY DO?

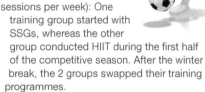

- 19 players from 4 youth teams (<16.5 years) of the 2 highest German divisions participated.

- Teams were randomly assigned to 2 training routines (2 endurance sessions per week): One training group started with SSGs, whereas the other group conducted HIIT during the first half of the competitive season. After the winter break, the 2 groups swapped their training programmes.

BEFORE AND AFTER THE TRAINING PERIODS

| Questionnaire | Creatine Kinase & Urea Concentrations | Vertical-jump height (CMJ & Drop Jump) | Straight Sprint & Change in Direction Performance | Small Sided Games | Endurance Testing |

WHAT DID THEY REPORT?

- Significant time effects were observed for individual anaerobic threshold (+1%), peak heart rate (-2%), and CMJ (-2%), with no significant interaction between groups.

- Players with low baseline individual anaerobic threshold values had greater improvements than those with high initial values (+4% vs +0%). A significant decrease was found for total recovery (-5%), and an increase was found far urea concentration (+9%).

CONCLUSION & PRACTICAL IMPLICATION

1. 4 weeks of in-season endurance training can lead to relevant, although only moderate adaptations in endurance capacity, particularly in players with low baseline levels. Players with an already well developed endurance capacity did not benefit from such additional intensive training.

2. Training effects were independent to the training method (SSG or HIIT).

3. From a sport-practical perspective it should be considered that HIIT needs only 63% of the total training time of SSGs.

4. Otherwise, SSGs enable the training of tactical and technical skills under conditions similar to the real game.

5. The slight decreases in CMJ height and total recovery together with the increase in urea concentration can be interpreted as early signs of fatigue due to additional intense exercise during the competition period. Thus, such training should he carefully applied in individuals who show recovery deficits, and the danger of over-taxing players must he taken into account.

CMJ = *Counter Movement Jump*

Designed by @YLMSportScience

49

OFF-SEASON

The off-season period is vital for recovery and regeneration. As players competing within European football teams may train and play continually over a 10 month period, it is vitally important that this phase of the year is focussed on achieving psychological, physical and physiological recovery and regeneration (Gamble, 2006; Wathen et al., 2000; Hawley and Burke, 1998). Additionally, according to Gamble (2006) based on the longevity engagement within structured training practices, common sense suggests that players should participate in unsupervised and off-site non-sport specific activity during the off-season. This unstructured, non-sport specific activity is suggested to have a psychological advantage through limiting the monotony of the training ground environment.

Strength Training

When discussing the strength training aspect of the off-season, Wathen et al., (2000) proposed that the inclusion of general non-sport specific strength training exercises are vitally important in order to apply a significant training variation that does not include certain lifts/exercises that are used extensively throughout the duration of the training year. General strength training, such as pulley or machine activities with single-joint exercises for the upper and lower body are more appropriate during this part of the training phase (Siff, 2002). Furthermore, cross-training methods and recreational sports are suggested as a better way of sustaining metabolic conditioning and body composition levels (Wathen et al, 2000).

Conditioning Levels

Maintaining conditioning levels and reducing the risk of increased body mass and fat levels is a fundamental part of the off-season. Due to the increased intensity and speed of play, coupled with the limited preparation period for elite players, it is of paramount importance they do not totally lose the physical benefits of the previous season's training.

According to Mujika and Padilla (2000), during the off-season period within elite level football, detraining is very apparent. Previous research has suggested that detraining is the partial or complete loss of training-induced adaptations in response to an insufficient training stimulus and that these detraining characteristics may be different depending on the amount of time without sufficient training (Hawley and Burke, 1998). According to Mujika and Padilla (2000), short-term cardiorespiratory detraining is characterised in highly trained athletes by a rapid reduction in **VO2max**, combined with reduced blood volume. The decline in both of these factors attributed to heart rate levels not increasing sufficiently during exercise to counter-balance the reduction in stroke volume and cardiac output. Due to this, physical performance is decreased (Mujika and Padilla, 2000).

For the off-season, the coaching staff could establish individual training schedules and nutritional guidance to the players. This would obviously depend on the length of the off-season period. Broadly, the players who have played most of the playing time of the season should be advocated to full recovery and "free" nutritional behaviour. The players with less playing time or relatively high percentages of body fat would resume endurance training sooner, and have their nutritional behaviour very well monitored.

Throughout the course of the season, technical coaches generally place a high training focus on both the technical and tactical components within training sessions, leaving the physical elements to be maintained through various sided games and tactical exercises. Recent literature however, has revealed how during the in-season, coaches can aim to improve the physical fitness profiles of the players and subsequent team performance, without significantly increasing the training volume, which may limit the fatigue related problems and possible overtraining syndrome (Dupont et al, 2004; Buchheit, 2008).

4. SPECIFIC TRAINING IN ELITE MODERN FOOTBALL

INTERMITTENT EXERCISES

Taking into consideration the fact that the nature of most team related sports is stop-start, performance in these intermittent sports has been likened more closely to speed, agility, strength and explosive power. This is so players train to perform short burst maximal exercise bouts, rather than focussing on developing the capacity to maintain continuous steady state submaximal bouts (Bangsbo, 1994). Individuals involved with the development of football players from a physical perspective should place a high priority on enhancing key physiological variables that significantly influence performance during intermittent sports (i.e. speed, agility, strength, endurance, power) through sport specific practices and maximal functional strength programmes (Hoff and Helgerud, 2004).

According to Dupont et al., (2004), developing endurance through short duration intermittent runs has shown improvements in *VO2max* levels and delayed fatigue in athletes. In addition, Balsom et al., (1992) indicated how short duration intermittent training limits blood lactate (*bLa*) production and increases *creatine phosphate (CrP)* metabolism during intermittent exercise, which is vitally important due to *CrP* (Impellizzeri et al, 2005) and muscle glycogen (Bishop et al, 2004) being described as the most important energy provider for this method of training.

According to Buchheit, (2008) running intensities of near maximal effort for short periods are generally individual, based on set thresholds of *maximal aerobic speed (MAS)*. Individual *MAS* is determined through analysis and indicated as the lowest running speed that elicits *VO2max* (Dupont et al, 2004; Leger and Boucher, 1980). Training methods inclusive of *MAS* are often composed of shuttle runs, aiming to introduce accelerations, decelerations and changes of direction, which are, as proposed by Buchheit, (2008) running patterns specific to intermittent sports, as well as being able to be adapted further for short anaerobic interval training sessions.

Furthermore, when discussing these fast, near maximal intensity training bouts that include decelerations and change of directions, previous literature has indicated that these exercises create acute hormonal responses and cause localised skeletal muscle damage (Vuorimaa et al, 1999; Kuoppasalmi et al, 1980; Clarkson et al, 1992; Kuipers, 1994). Muscle damage and fatigue related issues have been researched and reported by extensive examinations measuring the changes in serum myocellular proteins, such as creatine kinase (CK), myoglobin (Mb) and carbonic anyhdrase III (CA III) (Hortobagyi and Denahan, 1989; Komulainen et al, 1995). As suggested by Vuorimaa et al, (1999) endocrine research within this area has tended to focus on the hormonal changes of testosterone (i.e. the pituitary-testicular axis) and cortisol (adrenal cortex), luteinizing hormone (LH) and the follicle-stimulating hormone (FSH). Analysis of the hormonal secretions within these endocrine systems have been used to check the training status of athletes as part of overtraining monitoring (Adlercreutz et al., 1986) as well as determining the exercise-induced anabolic and catabolic activity which appears during and immediately after various bouts of exercise in numerous exercise protocols (Schwarz and Kinderman 1990; Vasankari et al. 1993).

Published research has shown that short duration intermittent running amongst elite football players has the potential to significantly improve the players' endurance and subsequent match performance (Bisciotti et al, 2000; Dupont et al, 2004). Findings from recent research with short intermittent runs of 15 seconds at 120% of *MAS* alternated with 15 seconds of passive recovery were successful in prompting and maintaining a high level of *VO2*. The study by Dupont et al, (2004) resulted in an 8.1% improvement in maximal aerobic speed (*MAS*) from 15.9 to 17.3 km per hour. The significant improvements developed through this training method (15 seconds at 120% *MAS*) allowed *VO2* to be sustained longer than

Football Conditioning: A Modern Scientific Approach

intermittent runs of 15 seconds at 110%, 130% and 140% of *MAS* or a continuous run at 100% of *MAS* (Dupont et al., 2002). Similar findings from Franch et al., (1998) suggested that short intermittent training bouts inclusive of 30 to 40 repetitions of 15 second runs alternated with 15 seconds of passive recovery performed 3 days per week over a 6 week period significantly increased the *MAS*. The role of *MAS* within elite level football should be highlighted and questioned as a functional football specific test based on the fact that players at the top level very rarely sustain high intensity running for periods long enough to induce *MAS*.

Showing similar findings to Dupont et al (2004), Simoneau et al (1985) found that short, high intensity intermittent training protocols separated with short recovery periods, allowed significant improvements in *VO2max* and the anaerobic capacity through positive influences of the physiological activity of aerobic and anaerobic pathways (Rodas et al, 2000; Tabata et al, 1996).

Although high-intensity anaerobic interval training is also regularly planned in the majority of team sports (Owen et al, 2012) with the aim of enhancing *VO2max* and the ability to reproduce maximal and near maximal exercise bouts (Hoff et al, 2005; Dupont et al, 2004). Glaister (2005) has suggested through extensive research that a relationship between *VO2max* and *repeated sprint ability (RSA)* is still not well established. This may be based on the fact that the role of *VO2max* within elite level football is still questionable due to the fact that high-speed actions are fundamentally involved with the outcome of the games, as opposed to sustained levels of aerobic work at a constant speed (Bangsbo, 1994). However, it has been shown that a greater aerobic capacity may play an important role within the recovery kinetics during high-intensity intermittent exercise (Tomlin and Wenger, 2002). Previous research has found a positive relationship between increased *VO2max* levels, game performance and increased high intensity running distance during a football match (Helgerud et al, 2001). In addition, Wong et al., (2009) showed that because explosive activities and aerobic endurance are important for football performance, it is of practical interest for coaches to simultaneously improve these capacities in their players.

Figure 18. Method for High-Intensity Intermittent Training (used by Dupont et al., 2004).

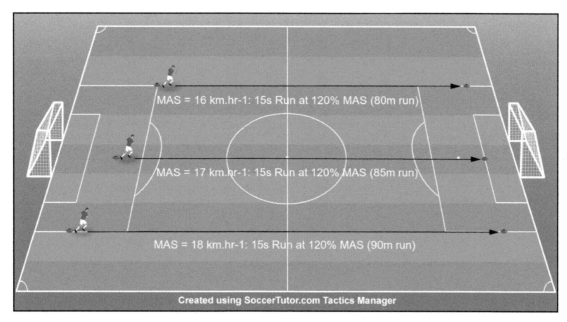

MAS = 16 km.hr-1: 15s Run at 120% MAS (80m run)

MAS = 17 km.hr-1: 15s Run at 120% MAS (85m run)

MAS = 18 km.hr-1: 15s Run at 120% MAS (90m run)

Created using SoccerTutor.com Tactics Manager

Football Conditioning: A Modern Scientific Approach

TRAINING PRINCIPLES / METHODS

Based on the literature discussed within this section and the information shown in *Table 6* (below) regarding intermittent training methods within football, it can be concluded that individuals involved with the physical development and training of players have various methods available when using intermittent exercises. These varying methods can be classified or inclusive of in-line running, changes of directions, with or without the ball. Previous research has attempted to show the physical, technical and psychological effects of implementing a range of these training methods with the aim of increasing the efficiency of the session. The physiological responses of traditional high-intensity intermittent exercise using in-line or straight-forward running have been well reported (Billat et al., 2002; Dupont et al., 2004). Subsequently, exercise patterns and physical profiles in football training and competitive match play suggest that players rarely move in straight lines over moderate or long distances. Due to these reported patterns and movement profiles reported, it would be more functional and sport specific to involve changes of direction as part of intermittent training sessions - training for the real demands of the game.

Table 6. Training Principles for the Use of Intermittent Exercise Used Within Football (from Dellal et al., 2010).

INTERMITTENT EXERCISE (WORK:REST IN SECONDS)	INTENSITY (% of Max Speed)	RECOVERY	SETS x REPS (mins)	NUMBER OF WORK PERIODS	NUMBER OF RECOVERY PERIODS	SHUTTLE DISTANCE USED
30:30 or 30:60	100%, 105% and 110%	Active (50% of Max)	1 (11 min 30s)	12	11	42m
15:15 or 15:30	100%, 105% and 115%	Passive	1 (9 min 45s)	20	19	30m
10:10 or 10:20	110%, 115% and 120%	Passive	2 (6 min 50s)	21	20	21m
5:5 or 5:10	Maximal	Active	2 (30s or 1 min)	6	20	13m

KEY POINTS:

1. *Individuals involved with the physical development of football players should place a high priority on enhancing key physiological intermittent variables that significantly influence performance (i.e. speed, agility, strength, endurance, power). This should be achieved through football specific practices and maximal functional strength programmes.*

2. *Developing endurance through short duration intermittent runs has shown improvements in VO2max levels and delayed fatigue.*

3. *As explosive activities and aerobic endurance are essential for football performance, it is of practical interest for coaches to simultaneously improve these capacities in their players.*

4. *Players rarely move in straight lines over moderate or long distances. Therefore, it would be more functional and sport specific to involve changes of direction as part of intermittent training sessions.*

CHANGES OF DIRECTION (COD)

The physiological influence of changes of direction (**COD**) or **shuttle runs (SR)** within bouts of intermittent running exercise is less known, especially in elite professional football training. The responses through **COD** or **SR** may be significantly different based on the need to accelerate, decelerate and the increased muscle involvement which is suggested to increase the internal load or heart rate response. Dellal et al., (2010) proposed a study with the aim of comparing the physiological impacts of intermittent exercise in specific shuttle running, which requires 180° changes of direction versus traditional in-line (**IL**) running. It was concluded that specific intermittent shuttle runs create a significantly higher physiological response than traditional in-line running. According to Dellal et al., (2010) the changes of direction are suggested to induce more anaerobic metabolism, and as a result create different responses compared with traditional in-line running. This specific study highlights the fact that coaches can be assured that when designing intermittent training programmes, the use of more specific movements inclusive of shuttle runs may be more functional and enhance the efficiency of the session.

Furthermore, the fact that intermittent training has previously been reported through in-line running without the use of the ball, literature discussing intermittent endurance training with the use of the ball is extremely limited. Having established that intermittent training inclusive of shuttle runs creates significantly greater physiological loads than in-line running, early research has also suggested that when possession of the ball is involved, the physiological cost of the movement increases (Reilly, 2003). According to Reilly (2003), when players run with close control of the ball, this changes the stride rate of the player and subsequently shortens their stride length when compared with normal running at the same speed. These mechanical changes are then suggested to be contributing to the increases in total energy cost of running with the ball (Reilly and Ball, 1984). Increasing or decreasing the stride length beyond individuals normal running stride then causes the O_2 consumption for a given speed to increase. Energy cost is also said to be increased further in matches when players perform irregular stride characteristics including feints or lateral cut movements to beat an opponent (Reilly, 2003; Reilly and Ball, 1984).

The review of literature within this section suggests that more appropriate, football specific, functional movements may be included in order to induce significantly greater physiological responses during intermittent running sessions. The involvement of **CODs** and possession of the ball should allow the training sessions not only to be more specific in relation to recreating the movement profile of players, but more importantly increases the motivation of the players within the training session from a psychological perspective.

KEY POINTS:

1. *When designing intermittent training programmes, the use of more specific movements may be more functional and enhance the efficiency of the session.*

2. *Running with the ball shortens the stride length compared to normal running at the same speed. These mechanical changes contribute to an increase in the total energy usage. The involvement of changes of direction and running with the ball allow the training sessions to be more specific in recreating the movements needed in a competitive game.*

3. *Football specific, functional movements will also elicit significantly greater physiological responses during intermittent running sessions.*

Figure 19. Physiological Responses to Running at Different Speeds With and Without the Ball
(Data from Reilly and Ball et al., 1984)

***** *Figure shows the increased energy cost of running with the ball, as opposed to running without the ball.*

GAME-RELATED ACTIVITIES

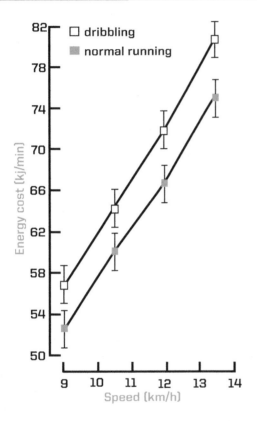

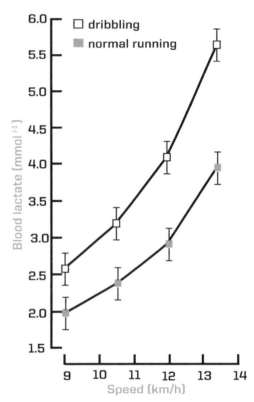

THE EFFECT OF LOW-VOLUME **SPRINT INTERVAL TRAINING (SIT)** ON THE DEVELOPMENT AND SUBSEQUENT MAINTENANCE OF AEROBIC FITNESS IN FOOTBALL PLAYERS

Tom W Macpherson & Matthew Weston
Int J Sport Perf Physiol, September 2014

The primary aim of this study was to examine the effectiveness of low-volume sprint interval training when used as replacement for regular aerobic training. It was a typical 2-week sprint interval training (**SIT**) intervention on the development of aerobic fitness in football players (part 1). A secondary aim was to examine the effect one **SIT** session per week had on the subsequent maintenance of aerobic fitness in football players (part 2).

In part 1, the 2 week **SIT** intervention had a small beneficial effect on the YoYo intermittent recovery test level 1 (**YYIRL1**) (+17 ± 11%), and **VO2max** (3.1 ± 5.0%), compared to the control group.

In part 2, one **SIT** session per week for 5 weeks had a small beneficial effect on **VO2max** (+4.2 ± 3.0%), with an unclear effect on **YYIRL1** (+8±16%).

PART 1 & PART 2

23 semi-professional players were in the study. 14 participated in a 2 week speed interval training intervention, with 9 in the control group. The **SIT** group performed 6 training sessions of 4-6 max 30 second sprints, replacing their regular aerobic training. The control group continued with their regular training.

Following this 2 week intervention, the **SIT** group were allocated to either intervention (7 players did 1 **SIT** session per week as replacement of regular aerobic training) or control (7 players did regular aerobic training with **no SIT** sessions) for a 5 week period.

TESTING

Pre and post measures were the YoYo intermittent recovery test level 1 (**YYIRL1**) and maximal oxygen uptake (**VO2max**).

CONCLUSIONS & PRACTICAL IMPLICATIONS

"2 weeks of **SIT** elicits small improvements in football players' high-intensity intermittent running performance and **VO2max**, therefore representing a worthwhile replacement of regular aerobic training. While physical considerations will always be secondary to a player's ability to fulfill their tactical/technical role on the pitch, inadequate physical preparation could limit a player's functioning during a match. However, physical preparation is frequently impaired by congested fixture schedules. Also, pressure on coaches to succeed can often result in injured players being hurried back to fitness. With such problems in mind, time-efficient training methods like **SIT** could have broad appeal in football, and other team sports, as **SIT** can provide a useful solution to the aforementioned complexities of training programme design."

Designed by @YLMSportScience

SPEED, REPEATED SPRINT ABILITY (RSA) AND AGILITY

Training for the Decisive Moments

According to Little and Williams (2005) the ability to produce a variety of explosive, high-speed movements has been indicated to significantly impact football match performance. Even though these high-speed actions only contribute to approximately 11% of the total distance covered (*TDC*) within a competitive match, at the elite level it is well documented that it is the short, explosive anaerobic events that generally constitute the more crucial game changing moments (e.g. sprint and shot, sprint into space to receive a pass, winning possession of the ball) (Rampinini et al, 2009). In order to train and enhance players' capacity to reproduce high speed actions, agility based movements within a competitive environment are needed, as well as understanding the recent literature which outlines the current trends. Recent research has proposed that high-speed or sprint actions within competitive football may be further categorised into more specific actions such as acceleration, maximal speed, agility (Little and Williams, 2005) and *RSA* (Girard et al, 2011).

Acceleration - Resistance Sled Pulls

Acceleration has been suggested as being the change in the rate of speed allowing players to reach upper thresholds of maximum velocity in a limited time. Many authors have reported improvements in acceleration through the use of different methods. For example, both Zafeiridis et al (2005) and Spinks et al (2007) have highlighted that resisted sprint work though sled pulling significantly improved acceleration performance (0-20 metres). Further analysis from the study by Spinks et al, (2007) revealed that a sled loading of approximately 10% of body mass does not appear to negatively affect acceleration kinematics, but ensures that there is still an adequate overload in the athlete's acceleration mechanics.

These acceleration improvements are aligned to the fact that there is an overload stimulus induced to acceleration mechanics and recruitment of the hip and knee extensors, resulting in greater application of horizontal power. Spinks et al (2007) also concluded that 10% of body mass used during sled pulls led to a decrease in first step ground contact time and an increased horizontal acceleration of arm swing which is a key component of acceleration phases in sprint development. Harrison and Bourke (2009) used resisted sled pulls with professional rugby players and with a load of 13% of body mass used 2 times a week for 6 weeks (6 x 20 metre sprints) which revealed a significant improvement over 5 metres, but showed no change over a 30 metre distance. Again, it suggests that resisted sled pulls lead to an increase in the acceleration phase, but just not over distances greater then 30 metres.

Example of Resisted Sprint Training Session

Maximal Strength Training

As indicated previously, when discussing the development of the acceleration phase within elite level professional football, not only resistance sled pulls have been researched. Many different methods have been used as an intervention to develop this key physical quality. The use of maximal strength training to develop speed and acceleration has been proposed by many authors (Wisloff et al, 2004; Wong et al, 2010). The reported strength, power and speed relationship has been supported through results gained from jumping, 10 and 30 metre sprint tests (Wisloff et al, 2004; Wong et al, 2010). Based on this information and current literature, it may be reasonable to suggest that increasing the players force of muscular contraction in football specific lower limb muscle groups, may result in increased acceleration and speed in skills critical to football such as turning, sprinting, and changing pace (McMillan et al, 2005). This is in line with Newton's 2nd law of motion and the relationship between force, mass (body weight + weighted sled) and acceleration.

FORCE = MASS x ACCELERATION (F = MA)

Few training intervention studies have been conducted at the elite level of professional football. One such study performed by Hoff and Helgerud (2002) concluded that an 8 week training intervention (3 training sessions per week) led to significant physical improvements. The aim of the study was to induce neural adaptations performing 4 sets of 5 repetitions using loads >85% of 1RM ensuring the emphasis throughout the movement was on maximal speed of movements. *A repetition maximum (RM) is the most weight you can lift for a defined number of repetitions e.g. 5RM would be the heaviest weight you could lift for 5 consecutive repetitions.*

The results of the intervention indicated an increase in 1RM half squats from 161 kg to 215 kg in a group of 8 players. In accordance to the increase in 1RM, the players showed an increase in rate of force development (*RFD*) of 52%. Furthermore, results from the sprint tests revealed a 10 metre improvement of 0.08 seconds, and performance over 40 metres showed an improvement of 0.13 seconds.

Helegrud et al, (2002) indicated that in another intervention performed amongst a Champions League team during preseason, (4 sets of 4 repetitions close to loads of 90% 1RM) over an 8 week period performing 2 sessions per week, the players improved their half squat 1RM from 116 kg to 176 kg. At the same time the 10 metre sprint results improved from 1.87 seconds to 1.81 seconds with the 20 metre sprint test improving from 3.13 seconds to 3.08 seconds.

Interestingly, these functional findings from Helgerud et al, (2002) and Hoff and Helgerud, (2002) draw some conflicting reports with other researchers surrounding this area. Many researchers do not support the view that fast, explosive movements within strength training is more effective than the traditional, slow weight training when trying to enhance muscle function. Within the investigation by Blazevich and Jenkins (2002), subjects trained for a 7 week period, lifting either 30-50% or 70-90% of 1RM for both the slow and fast speed groups. Results from the study revealed no significant differences in sprint performance, 1RM squat, hip extension or flexion torque between the two groups. It was however revealed that subjects from both groups showed significant improvements in each specific variable. Moreover, Young and Bilby (1993) compared the effect of slow vs. fast explosive squat performance over a 7.5 week period involving the subjects' training 3 times per week. Results from the study again, in line with previous research (Blazevich and Jenkins, 2002) showed significant increases in 1RM, peak isometric force, vertical jumps, thigh circumference and muscle thickness.

Maximum Speed

Maximum speed has been described as being the maximal velocity at which a player can sprint (Little and Williams, 2005) and speed is considered the most frequent action performed by either the scoring and/ or assisting player when preceding a goal (Faude et al, 2012). Little and Williams (2005) have suggested how superior performance in varied speed tests of professional players, compared with both the general population and the higher standards of

football, indicates that certain speed attributes are advantageous for elite football. Intuitively, fitness coaches regularly use speed-based drills, often favouring acceleration capacity, in order to replicate the short intense bouts during a game.

Assisted Training Methods

According to Ebben et al, (2008), assisted methods are inclusive of high-speed treadmill training, towing, and downhill sprinting, and are thought to increase running velocity by improving stride length or stride frequency (Hunter et al, 2004). Previous research suggests that assisted methods such as downhill sprinting may enhance the maximum running velocity (Costello, 1985), which was previously defined as a greater speed than which can be attained without assistance at a 0° slope (Facciono, 1994). Studies generally examining the use of downhill sprinting has included downhill slopes of approximately 3°. Recent research performed by Paradisis and Cooke (2006) indicated athletes that trained via a combination of uphill and downhill running on slopes of 3° significantly improved their 35 metre sprint performance when compared to the control group who trained on a 0° track. This particular study provides evidence that combined uphill-downhill training methods produced a 3.4% increase in maximal sprint speed alongside a 3.4% increase of stride frequency (no change in stride length). Further analysis revealed how the downhill training method produced a 1.1% improvement in maximum running speed and a 2.4% improvement in stride frequency (no change in stride length). Further research is needed on the use of hill work's influence on speed improvements, to clarify slope angles and distances.

Speed Testing

Within competitive match situations, it has been highlighted that the requirements of both acceleration and maximal speed capacities are vital due to the sprint distances recorded being anything between 1.5 and 105 metres (Little and Williams, 2005; Carling et al, 2008). According to individuals involved within the physical development who attempt to develop sport-

specific speed should be aware that repeated sprint ability (*RSA*), acceleration, maximum speed, and agility are distinct qualities and should be tested in isolation to produce performance improvements (Zafeiridis et al, 2005). Furthermore, for elite football players, when testing these components of speed a 10 metre test of acceleration, a flying 20 metre test of maximum speed, and a zig-zag test of agility would be appropriate in combination with specific component training (*RSA*, acceleration, agility, maximum speed).

Changes of Direction

It is vital for football players to produce explosive, powerful whole body movements inclusive of speed or directional changes, have the ability to change direction or start and stop quickly, plus any other specific movement that may involve a rapid change of direction (*COD*) (Sheppard et al, 2006; Markovic, 2007). According to Hewit et al (2010) these specific directional changes that involve players starting, stopping, twisting and turning can be defined as movement agility. What is clear from these suggestions regarding movement agility is that these movements include many factors and are comprised of 3 main components (Hewit et al, 2010):

- Technical

- Physical

- Perceptual

According to Bullock et al (2012) agility should be described as 'reactive agility' due to it requiring a combination of physical (e.g. speed, power, balance) and cognitive skills (e.g. decision making) that when developed in conjunction to each other, prove vital for successful performance in team sports.

Speed and Agility

Recently, speed, agility and quickness SAQ® training programmes have been developed and validated as an effective method to improve agility related actions in football (Polman et al, 2004; Pearson, 2001). The SAQ® method involves a system of progressive exercises aimed at developing key principles to enhance the capabilities athletes to be more skillful at higher speeds (Pearson et al, 2002). According to Bloomfield et al., (2007) this type of conditioning is thought to enable participants to react quicker to stimuli, accelerate quickly and more efficiently, and enhance their effectiveness of multi-directional movements. It is claimed that these improvements come through developing acceleration over short distances, deceleration and changes in direction, footwork patterns, movement responses, arm action, as well as linear, lateral, diagonal, and vertical movements (Brown et al, 2000). Although there are a few publications surrounding agility in football, there is a significant limitation in research regarding the use of agility training interventions at the elite level.

Repeated Sprint Ability (RSA)

Having discussed the benefits and methods used to develop the short, explosive bursts that are vitally important to the outcome of football games, the need to reproduce these movements time and time again throughout the duration of the match is vital. The importance of *RSA* is therefore an important fitness requirement, and subsequently understanding the specific training strategies that can improve this fitness component is of huge importance. Rampinini et al., (2007) established the validity of an *RSA* shuttle-running test (6 x 40 metre shuttle runs followed by 20 seconds of recovery between sprints) when revealing a significant relationship between total time to complete the *RSA* test and *high intensity distance covered (HIDC)* during a football match. Furthermore, this study indicated significant correlations between the performance in this *RSA* test and sprinting or *HIDC* during competitive matches at a professional level.

It is not too surprising to find that a limited amount of research have been published on training strategies

of *RSA*, as it is a complex fitness component that depends on both metabolic (e.g. oxidative capacity and phosphocreatine recovery) and neural factors (e.g. muscle activation and recruitment strategies) (Bishop et al, 2011). Researchers who have attempted to provide useful literature on the development of this area have generally made 2 key recommendations. When looking to develop *RSA* it is suggested to be important to include:

1. Some training to improve single-sprint performance/times inclusive of 'traditional' speed training and strength/power training.

2. The integration of high-intensity (85–90% *VO2max*) interval training with the aim of trying to improve the ability to recover between sprint bouts.

Recent research by Bravo et al (2007) compared the effects of high-intensity aerobic interval and repeated sprint ability (*RSA*) training on aerobic and anaerobic physiological variables in male football players. Within the study, the participants were randomly assigned into 2 groups:

1. **Interval Training (IT) Group** which consisted of 4 × 4 minutes running at 90–95% of *HRmax.*

2. **Repeated Sprint (RS) Training Group** which consisted of 3 × 6 maximal 40 metre shuttle sprints.

Findings from the study revealed how only the *RS* group showed improvements in the *RSA* tests when compared to the *IT* group. The improvement in *RSA* (average times) within the *RS* group does not appear to be influenced by enhanced aerobic fitness as both groups showed significant improvements in *VO2max*. According to Bishop and Edge (2006), although *RSA* may be partially related to aerobic power, the improvement in *RSA* average time may reflect enhanced anaerobic metabolism which is also an important determinant of *RSA* and can be increased with sprint training (Jacobs et al, 1987). This suggests an increase in overall anaerobic performance but not in the ability to recover between sprints.

61

KEY POINTS:

1. *Although sprinting only accounts for 11% of the running in a football match, it is much more prominent for the key moments in games. Speed is considered the most frequent action performed by either the scoring and/or assisting player when preceding a goal.*

2. *According to Ebben et al, (2008), assisted methods are inclusive of high-speed treadmill training, towing, and downhill sprinting, and are thought to increase running velocity by improving stride length or stride frequency.*

3. *When looking to develop RSA it is suggested to be important to include:*

   - *Some training to improve single-sprint performance/times inclusive of 'traditional' speed training and strength/power training.*

   - *The integration of high-intensity (85–90% VO2max) interval training with the aim of trying to improve the ability to recover between sprint bouts.*

Figure 20. Functional Model of Agility (from Hewit et al., 2010).

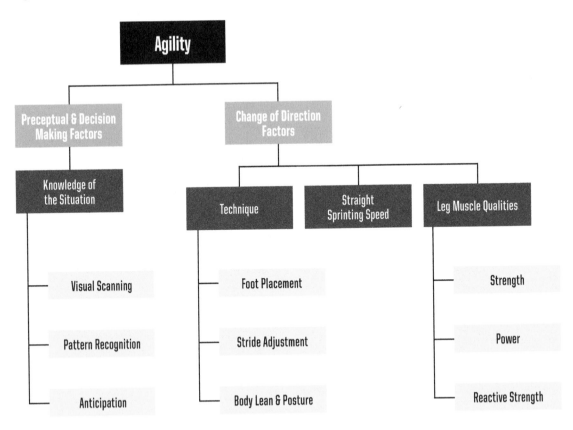

"Speed may be a generic quality, but the mechanical horizontal determinants of acceleration and maximal sprinting speed differ."

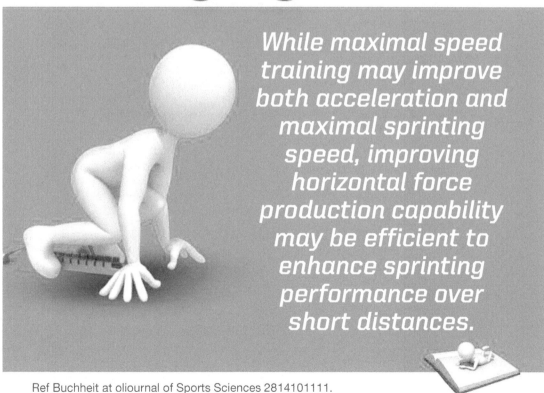

While maximal speed training may improve both acceleration and maximal sprinting speed, improving horizontal force production capability may be efficient to enhance sprinting performance over short distances.

Ref Buchheit at oliournal of Sports Sciences 2814101111.

Designed by @YLMSportScience

Repeated Sprint Ability: Recommendations for Training

Reference: Bishop, Girard & Mendez-Villanueva, Sports Medicine, 2011

1 A DETERMINANT FACTOR

Repeated sprint ability (RSA) is an important fitness requirement of team-sport athletes, and it is important to better understand training strategies that can improve this fitness component.

2 TWO THEORIES

In the absence of strong scientific evidence, 2 principal training theories have emerged. One is based on the concept of training specificity and maintains that the best way to train RSA is to perform repeated sprints. The second proposes that training interventions that target the main factors limiting RSA may be a more effective approach.

3 A COMPLEX COMPONENT

RSA depends on both metabolic (e.g. Oxidative capacity and PCr recovery) and neural factors (e.g. Muscle activation and recruitment strategies) among others.

TRAINING METHODS

4

Different training strategies can be used in order to improve each of these potential limiting factors, and in turn RSA.

5 KEY TRAINING PRINCIPLE #1

It is important to include some training to improve single-sprint performance. This should include (i) Specific Sprint Training; (ii) Strength/Power Training; and (iii) occasional High-intensity Training (e.g. Repeated, 30 seconds, all-out efforts separated by 10 minutes of recovery) to increase the anaerobic capacity.

6 KEY TRAINING PRINCIPLE #2

It is also important to include some interval training to best improve the ability to recover between sprints (if the goal is to improve fatigue resistance). High-intensity (80-90%VO2max) interval training, interspersed with rest periods that are shorter than the work periods is efficient at improving the ability to recover between sprints by increasing aerobic fitness (VO2max and the lactate threshold), and the rate of PCR resynthesis .

Designed by @YLMSportScience

SMALL SIDED GAMES

The suggestion that small sided games (*SSGs*) may simulate the physiologic workloads and intensities of actual match play while also developing technical and tactical proficiency has led to its popularity as a training method in the applied and scientific domain within recent years (Dellal et al, 2011; Owen et al, 2012). From an applied perspective, the potential to enhance players' aerobic capacity through game related movements inclusive of ball involvement, may increase the motivation of all individuals involved with the development of elite professional football players. Therefore, the advantages of the use of *SSGs* rather than generic 'traditional' training methods such as interval or continuous running training are quite apparent. However, manipulating the pitch size, number of games played, duration, coach encouragement, and technical restrictions have been shown to severely alter the physical and technical demands associated with *SSGs* (Owen et al., 2004;

Owen et al, 2011; Rampinini et al, 2007; Hill-Hass et al, 2011). Recently there has been a significant increase in the number of papers published regarding the use of *SSGs* as a physical preparation tool and the functional role they may play within elite professional football.

Contemporary findings comparing the effects of small sided games (*SSGs*) in football vs. high-intensity intermittent training (*HIT*) on a continuous and intermittent performance. It demonstrated both training interventions are equally effective in developing the aerobic capacity and the ability to perform intermittent exercises with changes of direction (*COD*) in male amateur players. Furthermore, these two methods of training over 6 weeks may induce similar effects on the recovery capacity, as well as enhancing a player's ability to reproduce 180° *COD*. As a result of this study, coaches can be confident in using either training method to achieve the specific

Table 7. The Experimental Design of Dellal (et al., 2012).

WEEK	MONDAY	TUESDAY	WEDNESDAY	THURSDAY	FRIDAY	SATURDAY	SUNDAY
Block 1							
1		Vameval	Tech-Tact		Tech-Tact		Match
2		Tech-Tact	30-15 IFT	Tech-Tact		Match	
Block 2							
3		**Session 1:** 2v2 or 30s-30s	**Session 2:** 2v2 or 30s-30s		Tech-Tact		Match
4		Tech-Tact	**Session 3:** 2v2 or 30s-30s		Tech-Tact		Match
5		**Session 4:** 2v2 or 15s-15s	**Session 5:** 2v2 or 15s-15s	Tech-Tact		Match	
6		Tech-Tact	**Session 6:** 2v2 or 15s-15s		Tech-Tact		Match
7		**Session 7:** 2v2 or 10s-10s	**Session 8:** 2v2 or 10s-10s	Tech-Tact		Match	
8		Tech-Tact	**Session 9:** 2v2 or 10s-10s		Tech-Tact		Match
Block 3							
9		Tech-Tact	Vameval		Tech-Tact		Match
10		Tech-Tact	30-15 IFT		Tech-Tact		Match

objective of the training session and optimise the training itself.

In addition to Dellal et al (2012), regarding the comparison of intermittent vs. *SSGs* training on physical performance, a previous study also examined the differences between *HR* responses within and between short-duration intermittent running and *SSGs* amongst elite level professional football players (Dellal et al, 2008). To conclude, the findings showed how specific *SSGs* create similar increased *HR* responses to the same level as achieved within short-duration intermittent running. These findings are vitally important and extremely useful as it highlights the fact that the use of a *SSGs* training can be used to add variety during training sessions that allow the integration of physical, technical, and tactical components, whilst achieving the same intensity of short-duration intermittent running.

Based on previous research suggesting that *SSGs* create similar physical responses to those manifested within intermittent running training, examining the effects of different bout durations during *SSGs* may only assist in developing improved training adaptations. Franchini et al (2010) investigated various bout durations within *SSGs* (3 v 3 + goalkeepers) with the aim of highlighting whether or not the increase in bout duration would affect the exercise intensity and technical actions amongst male football players. It was concluded that the increases in bout duration from 2 to 6 minutes resulted in decreased intensity between the 4 and 6 minute games. However, the varying durations did not influence the technical actions and proficiency.

According to Franchini et al (2010) the variance in *HR* change (4 minute games = 89.5% *HRmax* vs. 6 minute games = 87.8% *HRmax*) is probably not enough to induce different training adaptations, leading to the concept that coaches may use different bout durations with minimal impact on exercise intensity and without compromising technical proficiency. The reduction in the longer bout durations may be as a cause of fatigue, suggesting that for 3 v 3 + goalkeepers, *SSGs* any longer than 4 minutes in length to induce high-intensity intermittent aerobic adaptations may be

questionable, although further research is needed to clarify this.

Having described the findings from Franchini et al., (2010) regarding the effect of bout durations, Owen et al (2012) examined the effects of a 4 week small sided game (3 minute - 3 v 3 + goalkeepers) training intervention over 7 sessions on the physical performance (i.e., speed, aerobic performance, and repeated sprint ability) of elite male football players during the in-season break. The main findings from the investigation revealed that:

- The training intervention significantly improved players' repeated sprint ability and sprint performance (total sprint time and % reduction).

- It also significantly improved the running economy (*CR*), which was presented as a reduction in *VO2* and *HR* when running at submaximal levels.

- Additionally, it appeared from the findings of Owen et al (2012) that the periodized small sided game intervention could have a positive effect on both the anaerobic and aerobic system during the in-season break.

Overall, this section concludes that findings from the research conducted on *SSGs* may add to the emerging paradigm of research identifying *SSGs* as an alternative training method to generic drills (e.g. interval running training) for improving physical fitness characteristics in elite senior football players. However, it should be noted that although *SSGs* recreate the high-intensity demands of competitive matches from an aerobic perspective, previous and current literature has suggested that the development of high-speed capabilities and sprint distance is questionable due to the limitations of pitch sizes used (Owen et al, 2013; Casamichana and Castellano, 2010).

Table 8. Average Percentage of HR Reserve (%HRres) *During Different Sided Games and During the Different Short-Duration Intermittent Running Sessions* (Dellal et al., 2008).

SMALL SIDED GAMES					
1 v 1	**2 v 2**	**4 v 4 + GK**	**8 v 8 + GK**	**8 v 8**	**10 v 10 + GK**
% HRres 77.60	80.10	77.10	80.30	71.70	75.70
Intersubject CV (%) 11.12	10.83	13.87	15.60	8.79	10.40

INTERMITTENT RUNNING					
10-10 110% VO$_2$max PR	**30-30 100% VO$_2$max PR**	**30-30 100% VO$_2$max PR**	**15-15 100% VO$_2$max PR**	**5-20 120% VO$_2$max PR**	–
% HRres 85.8	77.2	85.7	76.8	80.2	–
Intersubject CV (%) 4.50	5.97	5.27	5.20	8.50	–

CV = Coefficient of Variation

This *shows the average variation of the players tested within this type of session. The greater the value, the greater the variation of intensity per player. There is less variation when performing running drills vs. training games, however similar heart rate responses and greater motivation occur when using sided games. This may also be as a result of positional differences within the games.*

Figure 21. Heart Rate (HR) Example of 8 x 3 Minute Small Sided Games (3 v 3 + Goalkeepers).
* Player competing at Champions League level and international competitions

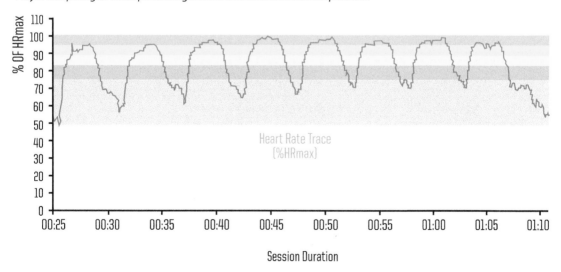

Table 9. Average Exercise Intensity (% HRmax) (Franchini et al., 2010).
* The data shown excludes the first minute of each bout
SD = Standard Deviation (statistical difference from the average)

	2 MIN DURATION		4 MIN DURATION		6 MIN DURATION		POOLED DATA	
	Average	SD	Average	SD	Average	SD	Average	SD
Bout 1	88.0	3.4	88.9	3.4	87.3	3.5	88.1	3.4 *
Bout 2	88.7	3.2	89.7	3.1	88.5	3.3	89	3.2 **
Bout 3	88.8	2.9	89.9	2.5	87.7	3.2	88.8	3.0 *
Bout 4	88.5	3.2	89.5	3.1	87.8	2.8 ***		

Table 10. Small Sided Game Training Intervention (Owen et al., 2012).
* All SSGs were 3 v 3 (+GKs) for a 3 minute duration with a 2 minute passive recovery

SESSION PROGRESSION	PROGRESSIVE OVERLOAD	TOTAL SSG DURATION (min)
SSGs 1	5 x 3 min games	15
SSGs 2	6 x 3 min games	18
SSGs 3	7 x 3 min games	21
SSGs 4	8 x 3 min games	24
SSGs 5	9 x 3 min games	27
SSGs 6	10 x 3 min games	30
SSGs 7	11 x 3 min games	33

CHAPTER SUMMARY

CHAPTER SUMMARY

PERIODIZATION

- Interest, research and application of specific training methods to reproduce the technical and physical demands of competitive match play has become more evident.

- Understanding the basic concept of training periodization and its 'load-recovery' concept (the 'super compensation theory') is of paramount importance.

- Although it is important for coaches to understand the concept of periodization for the preparation and early season stage, it is very difficult to administer within the season due to the variation of the training week, recovery periods and competitive fixtures.

THE DIFFERENCE BETWEEN 1 OR 2 GAMES PER WEEK

- Larger squads, player rotation, injury prevention techniques and improved recovery strategies have the primary aim of reducing the injury rate during periods with congested match fixtures is essential.

- Ensuring the non-playing squad and substitutes competitive match minutes lost are replaced in the correct manner and at the right time (e.g. reserve games, high speed and high intensity training) is of huge importance as these players become important players as the season progresses.

PRE-SEASON TRAINING

- Throughout pre-season, ensure the focus is placed on the key football specific muscle groups and energy systems to improve endurance, strength, speed and power.

- Coaches can aim to improve the physical fitness profiles of the players and subsequent team performance, without significantly increasing the training volume which may increase fatigue/injury problems.

- During the pre-season period, concurrent muscular strength and high-intensity interval running training can be used in order to enhance professional football players' explosive performance in conjunction to their intermittent and continuous aerobic endurance.

- If sport science, technical and medical staff do not plan the micro and meso-cycle pre-season training phase in advance with a gradual progressive overload to increase the physical capabilities of players, then more injuries may be sustained. As a result, players who do not complete pre-season periods have a higher risk of sustaining further injures during the in-season period.

IN-SEASON TRAINING

- Opposition quality, number of training days between matches, as well as any travelling associated with the fulfilment of fixtures, should influence the weekly or monthly training intensity. Understanding these factors as a combination may assist as a guide when planning the weekly or monthly training activity.

- First team players with the highest match availability and game time across the season post the highest levels of aerobic fitness (*VO2max*) in the middle of the season, while substitute players with less playing time score highest at the end of the season.

The reduction in volume of high-intensity training through the mid-season phase links to the long term plan, ensuring maximal fitness and freshness by avoiding any accumulative fatigue-induced injuries in the preparation of competitive fixtures

SPECIFIC TRAINING IN ELITE MODERN FOOTBALL

- Short-duration, high intensity intermittent running bouts amongst elite football players has been shown to significantly improve the players' endurance and subsequent match performance.

- Greater player motivation, sport specific muscular recruitment and a higher energy demand are suggested when changes of direction (*COD*) and ball possession is included within training strategies versus traditional in-line running bouts.

- When designing intermittent training programmes, the use of more specific movements may be more functional and enhance the efficiency of the session.

- Running with the ball shortens the stride length compared to normal running at the same speed. These mechanical changes contribute to an increase in the total energy usage. The involvement of changes of direction and running with the ball allow the training sessions to be more specific in recreating the movements needed in a competitive game.

- Football specific, functional movements will elicit greater physiological responses during intermittent running sessions.

- Although sprinting only accounts for 11% of the running in a football match, it is much more prominent for the key moments in games. Speed is considered the most

frequent action performed by either the scoring and/or assisting player when preceding a goal.

REPEATED SPRINT ABILITY (RSA)

- When looking to develop *RSA* it is suggested to be important to include 1) Training to improve single-sprint performance inclusive of 'traditional' speed training and strength/power training, and 2) High-intensity interval training with the aim of trying to improve the ability to recover between sprints.

- Increasing players' lower body force production results in increased acceleration and speed in skills critical to football such as turning, sprinting, and changing pace.

- Techniques used to enhance speed include resisted (e.g. strength training, weight sled pulls) or assisted running (e.g. treadmill training, towing, and downhill sprinting).

- Producing explosive, powerful whole-body movements inclusive of speed or changes of direction (*COD*) in response to a sport specific stimulus improves the ability to change direction or start and stop quickly, plus any other specific movements that may be vital.

Football Conditioning: A Modern Scientific Approach

SHORT INTENSIVE TRAINING (SIT)

- 2 weeks of *SIT* elicits small improvements in football players' high-intensity intermittent running performance and VO2max, therefore representing a worthwhile replacement of regular aerobic training.

- While physical considerations will always be secondary to a player's ability to fulfill their tactical/technical role on the pitch, inadequate physical preparation could limit a player's functioning during a match.

- Physical preparation is frequently impaired by congested fixture schedules. Also, pressure on coaches to succeed can often result in injured players being hurried back to fitness.

- With such problems in mind, time-efficient training methods like SIT could have broad appeal in football, as it can provide a useful solution to the aforementioned complexities of training programme design.

Football Conditioning: A Modern Scientific Approach

CHAPTER 2

SMALL SIDED GAMES

SMALL SIDED GAMES

1. **Physical and Physiological Demands of Small Sided Games (SSGs)**

   - Match Play and Comparisons to *SSGs*

   - Physical Developments within *SSGs*

2. **Variables Affecting SSGs Intensity**

   - Pitch Area

   - Player Numbers

   - Concurrent Effects of Pitch Area and Player Numbers

   - Rule Changes;
     (a) Variations of Game Performance Outcomes
     (b) Collective Ball Possession
     (With vs Without Directional Play)
     (c) Coach Encouragement
     (d) Inclusion of Goalkeepers
     (e) Duration and Number of Bouts

3. **Periodization of Small Sided Games**

4. **Workload Evaluation During Small Sided Games**

5. **Limitations of Small Sided Games**

Throughout the last few years there has been a significant increase in research surrounding the use of *SSGs* within all levels of football from youth, amateur, university and professional. The development and application of football related sport science methods, along with the improvement of equipment providing better monitoring and analysis of training methods may be linked to the increased attention *SSGs* have received.

Trying to maximise player's physical, technical and tactical abilities is of paramount importance, therefore making *SSGs* an appealing method. Using *SSGs* as a multi-functional training purpose may potentially allow for the development of many key football components within a limited time period, however, further research concerning the benefits of these games is warranted in order to maximise the application of them and allow players to compete at the highest possible level.

To date, current literature examining the effects of specific-sided games have revealed how physiological (e.g. heart rate, blood lactate levels and rate of perceived exertion), technical and tactical elements can be significantly altered if components such as the number of players, pitch dimensions, game rules and coach encouragement are varied.

In order to develop the research findings, additional research is needed to work towards developing the optimum use of *SSGs* and the role they play within the preparation of players competing at the elite level of the professional game.

1. PHYSICAL AND PHYSIOLOGICAL DEMANDS OF SMALL SIDED GAMES

PHYSICAL AND PHYSIOLOGICAL DEMANDS OF SMALL SIDED GAMES

Previous research has indicated that key physical, physiological, social, psychological, technical and tactical factors can influence the performance of football players (Clemente et al., 2012; Bangsbo, 1994). Integration of these factors is vitally important if the focus is to significantly and directly influence performance over time. Furthermore, according to Jones and Drust (2007), the design process of training programmes should consider the integration of all these factors (Jones and Drust, 2007).

The findings of Dellal et al., (2010) and Reilly and Ball, (1984) have concluded that more functional football specific physical and physiological developments can be conducted and has subsequently led to increased published work researching the use of various sided games (Casamichana and Castellano, 2010; Franchini et al., 2010).

Literature surrounding the training methods at the elite level have promoted the notion that specific football developments are attained when the training recreates the competitive demands from a technical, tactical and physical perspective (Owen et al., 2011; Mallo and Navarro, 2008; Clemente et al., 2012; Owen et al., 2004). One way to reproduce the competitive demands within a training environment is through the use of small sided games.

However, for the development and integration of *SSGs* to be maximised as a conditioning or preparation tool, it is vitally important to have an increased understanding of their effects from a physical, physiological, technical, tactical and psychological perspective.

According to Clemente et al., (2012) recent studies within the area have systematically investigated the effects on players when altering different variables or game rules, including pitch size (Kelly and Drust, 2009; Owen et al., 2004; Tessitore et al., 2006), the impact of specific tactical zones (Dellal et al., 2008; Mallo

and Navarro, 2008), varying the number of players (Williams and Owen, 2007; Katis and Kellis, 2009), and the duration and recovery times included when using *SSGs* (Dellal et al., 2012).

KEY POINT:

Specific football developments are attained when the training recreates the competitive demands from a technical, tactical and physical perspective. One way to reproduce the competitive demands within a training environment is through the use of small sided games.

Football Conditioning: A Modern Scientific Approach

PHYSIOLOGICAL RESPONSES AND ACTIVITY PROFILES OF SMALL SIDED GAMES (SSG)

Physiological and Perceptual Responses

Higher in the smaller SSG formats (2 v 2 and 3 v 3).

Practical Implications for Coaches

Coaches can use lower numbers of players (2 and 3-a-side) to increase cardiovascular demands but higher number of players (4 and 5-a-side) to increase variability and specificity. Activity profile and body load were not as different as expected, however, 4-a-side SSGs presented higher values and higher variability, while the 3 v 3 SSG was the most stable format.

Aerobic Fitness Development

2 v 2 and 2 v 3 may be useful for training to improve aerobic fitness in football players because they can elicit heart rate responses around 90% of maximal heart rate.

What About 4 and 5-a-side?

This could indicate that smaller formats (2 v 2 and 2 v 3) are more appropriate to increase physiological stress, whereas larger formats (4 v 4 and 5 v 5) can be used to improve match specific demands.

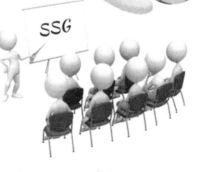

REFERENCE
M. Aguiar, G. Botelho, B. Goncalves and J. Sampaio
J Strength Cond Research, December 2014

Designed by @YLMSportScience

MATCH PLAY AND COMPARISONS TO SMALL SIDED GAMES

In order to develop *SSGs* within the training structure of clubs, it is of paramount importance that the physical activities are compared between *SSGs* and competitive matches. One of the first studies investigating the physiological and physical comparisons between *SSGs* and competitive matches was performed by Owen et al., (2004). Findings from this study revealed how a 3 v 3 *SSG* induced similar heart rate (*HR*) responses to those within competitive match play as shown below (*Figure 22*). In addition, Casamichana and Castellano (2010) examined the physical, physiological, motor responses and perceived exertion during 3 different *SSG* sessions amongst academy players. During the different *SSGs*, the 3 different playing areas were 275m², 175m² and 75m²

respectively while the number of players per team remained constant (5 v 5 + GKs). Findings from the study concluded that within the larger area, the physical variables including total distance covered, high intensity distance covered, maximum speed, work-to-rest ratio and number of sprints increased. It was also revealed that the physiological workload reported and the rate of perceived exertion (*RPE*) were all significantly higher, while certain technical variables such as interceptions, control, dribbles, shots at goal and clearances were lower. Overall, this particular study highlights that the size of pitch should be taken into consideration when planning specific *SSGs* as part of the training structure, as it significantly influences the physical and technical involvement.

Figure 22. Heart Rate Response of SSGs and Comparisons to 11 v 11 Match Play (Owen et al., 2004, Insight).

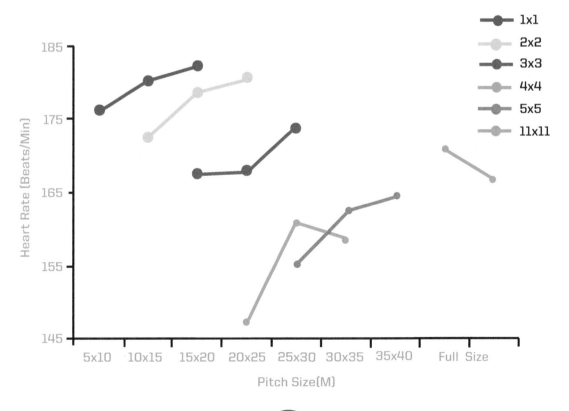

Interestingly, when comparing the findings of Casamichana and Castellano (2010) with similar studies involving **SSGs** of similar duration periods or against competitive matches, it has been suggested that the variable *'distance covered per minute'* or *'meterage per minute (m/min)'* is representative of the general intensity experienced by a player within these activities, therefore can be used as a global index of task/game intensity.

Recent research has shown **SSGs** range from 87 m/min on smaller pitches to 125 m/min on larger pitches with the same number of players (Casamichana and Castellano, 2010). These findings are consistent with previous reports surrounding **SSGs** suggested by Pereira et al., (2007) who found that young Brazilian football players covered:

- 118 m/min in the under 15 category.
- 105 m/min in the under 17 category.
- 109 m/min in the under 19 category.
- In addition, a study conducted by Barbero-Alvarez et al (2007) indicated that Spanish pre-teen players covered an average of 100 m/min.

Interestingly Owen et al (2013) revealed that **SSGs** induce a significantly greater or faster playing speed when compared to medium sided games (**MSGs**) and large sided games (**LSGs**). Furthermore, the metres covered per minute of play between the games were significantly different showing **SSGs** with the highest meterage values (198.5 m/min) when compared to medium sided games (**MSGs**) (106.9 m/min) and large sided games (**LSGs**) (120.4 m/min).

The fact the faster speed of play has been associated with the **SSGs** may be due to the smaller pitch sizes and limited time in possession of the ball due to the close proximity of opponents, compared to larger sided games. Findings from Owen et al (2103) revealed that as the number of players increases from **SSGs** to **MSGs**, to **LSGs**, the speed of play decreases due to less pressure from opponents, increased pitch sizes and more passing options which ensures the players can limit the amount of running they perform. However, **SSGs** and **MSGs** do not induce high speed movements when compared to **LSGs** which are similar to competitive matches. Discussing the metres covered per minute within **SSGs** and the comparisons between competitive matches or **LSGs** as within the study by Owen et al (2013), recent literature suggests that elite professional players cover distances of 9-12 km per 90 minute match. Generally, irrespective of positional roles, games are played at an average speed of 111.11 m/min to 133.33 m/min. In light of this, when the focus is to train at 'game intensity', coaches should ensure training games induce a speed of play equal to or greater than 111.11 m/min.

In a more specific and detailed investigation into the comparisons between **SSGs** and **LSGs** (11 v 11), Dellal et al (2012) monitored the effects of commonly used rule changes (free play; 1 touch; 2 touch) on the technical and physical demands among elite professional football players. Within the study 5 different playing positions during 4 minute **SSGs** were compared against the same players and positions competing in the **LSGs** (11 v 11). Findings from the study reported:

- Significantly higher heart rate (**HR**) values in **SSGs** when compared to match play for all playing positions.
- Lower rate of perceived exertion (**RPE**) values during free play possession based **SSGs** for defensive midfielders, wide midfielders and forwards.
- 4 v 4 **SSGs** played with a limitation of 1 or 2 touches increased the high-intensity running and the difficulty to perform technical actions which is arguably more specific to match demands.

Consequently, coaches need to fully understand the different physiological demands imposed upon players within **SSGs**, especially if they include rule changes in relation to ball possession within the session. Additionally, coaches should also have an understanding regarding the physical, physiological and technical differences between positional roles.

Figure 23. An Example of Positional Differences (Metres per Minute) *of an International Team During a* **Competitive World Cup Qualifying Fixture** (unpublished data).

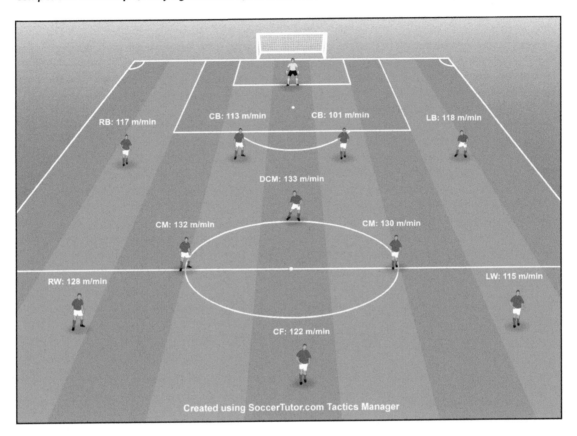

PHYSICAL DEVELOPMENTS WITHIN SMALL SIDED GAMES

Developing a better understanding of physiological and technical demands imposed on players within **SSGs** allows the opportunity to further analyse the movement profiles of players. At most levels, performing repetitive sprint efforts, changes of direction, shooting, tackling and dribbling are fundamental components and efforts needed to compete. However, these specific movements and actions within **SSGs** result in severely strain through additional loading placed on football specific muscle groups. This additional load imposed upon players may offer an may offer an additional physical stimulus because the ability to perform technical and tactical requirements under fatigued conditions is considered important for football (Iaia et al, 2009).

Dellal et al (2011) examined the relationship between playing levels in football (amateur vs. professional) using various **SSGs** (2 v 2; 3 v 3; 4 v 4). The main findings revealed significant differences between elite and amateur players concerning their ability or capacity to perform high-intensity actions, in combination with their competency to execute various technical abilities. Further analysis from the investigation showed how amateurs completed less successful passes, produced higher **RPE** and **bLa** values and less sprint distance and high intensity running. The comparison of the professional and amateur football players' activities during **SSGs** showed that the playing level influences the physiological responses, physical output and technical activities.

Table 11. Physical and Technical Demands of SSGs (3 v 3) Among Professional Football Players (Dellal et al., 2011).

	PHYSICAL AND TECHNICAL DEMANDS IN A PROFESSIONAL 3v3 SSG (N=20)			
	1 Touch	2 Touches	Free Play	Average
Total Distance (m)	22476.6	2124.7	2014.0	2128.8
Total Distance Sprinting (m)	397.0	351.2	315.6	354.6
% of Total Distance Sprinting	17.7	16.6	15.7	16.7
Total Distance in HIR (m)	523.2	473.9	422.5	473.2
% of Total Distance in HIR (m)	23.4	22.4	21.1	22.3
Number of Duels	30.9	28.2	26.8	28.6
Number of Duels per minute	2.6	2.3	2.2	2.4
% of Successful Passes	52.1	69.9	71.7	64.5
Total Number of Ball Losses	17.1	15.2	14.4	15.5
Number of Ball Losses per minute	1.4	1.3	1.2	1.3
Total Distance in Possession	51.8	43.8	41.7	45.8

The Effect of Pitch Size

It is well reported that physical demands during **SSGs** can be significantly influenced through the manipulation of key variables such as player numbers, pitch area size, possession rule changes and bout durations (Casimichana and Castellano, 2010; Dellal et al, 2011; Owen et al, 2004; Owen et al, 2011). Recent research within varying levels of football has revealed that changing the dimensions of the training pitch can create significantly different physiological and movement profiles. It should be noted however, that the various studies investigating the effects of the pitch dimensions on the players suggested contrasting opinions. One such study researching the effects of changing pitch sizes suggested that no significant

Football Conditioning: A Modern Scientific Approach

differences between *HR* responses were observed when *SSGs* were played on 3 different dimensions (Kelly and Drust, 2008), whereas contrasting findings revealed significant differences in *HR* responses between *SSGs* played on different dimensions. Increased *HR* values have been reported during *SSGs* when played on larger sized pitches, compared to smaller dimensions (Owen et al, 2004; Rampinini et al, 2007; Casamichana and Castellano, 2010).

According to Kelly and Drust (2008), the organisation of training sessions should ensure that pitch sizes should be carefully considered in order to achieve the training objective. If the main target of the session is to develop physical and technical components in isolation or in conjunction to each other, then the correct pitch sizes must be utilised. Owen et al (2004) suggested that manipulation of pitch dimensions can directly affect the training intensity, which is in agreement with the later findings proposed by Tessitore et al (2006) who also indicated that the intensity of training sessions can be increased or decreased based on varying the pitch dimensions. Furthermore, Tessitore et al (2006) indicated that smaller playing surfaces (irrespective of player

numbers) result in increasing exercise intensity from 61% to 76% of players' *VO2max*.

Within a similar investigation, Rampinini et al (2007) found higher blood lactate (*bLa*) values during different *SSG* formations played on a larger pitch, when compared to medium and small sized pitches. These findings concurred with Tessitore et al (2006) who concluded that 6 v 6 games played on bigger pitches (50 x 40 yards) resulted in significantly higher aerobic activity. Previous studies have recently performed research investigating the effects of pitch dimensions on the rate of perceived exertion (*RPE*) (Rampinini et al, 2007; Casamichana and Castellano, 2010). On both occasions it was concluded that there were significant differences when comparing medium and large pitches, both of which resulted in higher *RPE* ratings when compared to smaller pitches.

Later within this chapter, the author will explain the effects of a periodized approach to *SSGs* and also how using small, medium and large sided games can potentially assist in the development of the majority of physical demands imposed within competitive match play (e.g. high intensity running, sprinting).

Figure 24. Total Distance Covered in Relation to High Intensity Running (HIR) and Sprint Distance Comparisons Between Playing Level (Amateur vs. Professional) Using SSGs (from Dellal et al., 2011).

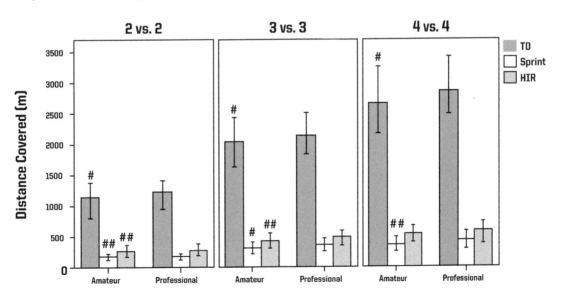

Physiological Demands

Having highlighted the physical profiles of players with respect to distance covered and relative speed thresholds defined within the movement patterns, the physiological demands induced by **SSGs** such as heart rate (**HR**) response, blood lactate levels (**bLa**) and internal load are revealed through reported session rate of perceived exertion (**RPE**). These values are fundamental in order to further understand the role these games play within elite professional football training.

The physiological responses of adult football players have provided evidence that **SSGs** elicit **HR** responses approximately 85-95% of **HRmax** (Hoff et al, 2002; Kelly and Drust, 2009) which may lead to improvements in aerobic fitness and subsequent match performance (Helgerud et al., 2001; Impellizzeri et al., 2006). One of the most recent reports regarding **HR** monitoring within **SSGs** revealed that professional and amateur level players expressed similar **%HRmax** and **%HRres**

responses (Dellal et al, 2011). As mentioned previously, the author of this study attributed the key difference between playing level to be the speed of movements within the **SSGs** (**HI** running and sprinting) - shown in **Figure 24** on the previous page.

Recently, Owen et al (2011) examined the differences between **HR** responses and technical activities on elite European level players when exposed to 2 different sided training games:

- **SSGs** = 3 v 3 + GKs in 30 x 25 yard area.
- **LSGs** = 9 v 9 + GKs in 60 x 50 yard area.

The results show that **SSGs** led to significantly higher **HR** responses compared to the **LSGs** (**Figure 25** below). During **SSGs**, players spent significantly longer in the **>85% maximal HR zone** compared to **LSGs** which matches previous research (Hoff et al, 2002; Kelly and Drust, 2009; Dellal et al, 2010), that showed that **SSGs** can induce **HR** responses to sufficient intensities in order to enhance aerobic capacity.

Figure 25. Heart Rate Response Comparison Between SSGs (3 v 3 + GKs) and LSGs (9 v 9 + GKs).

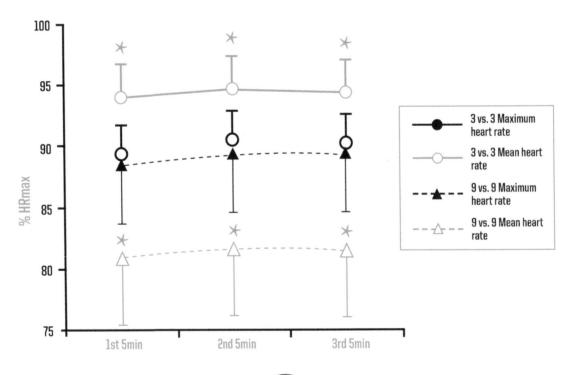

Additionally, a specific study was performed by Hoff et al (2002), determining whether small groups or **SSGs** are an appropriate intervention for interval training among elite professional football players and whether **HR** in football specific training is a valid measure of actual work intensity. The outcome of the study revealed that the exercise intensity from the **SSGs** (4 v 4 + GKs) was 91.3% of **HRmax** or 84.5% of **VO2max**. Furthermore, the corresponding intensity generated from the dribbling track was 93.5% of **HRmax** or 91.7% of **VO2max**. **Figure 26** (below) highlights the relationship between **HR** and **VO2**

submaximal intensities measured during an incremental laboratory treadmill test. The heart rate-VO2 relationship described within previous chapters of this book indicated that **SSGs** were not significantly different from running on the treadmill, however the dribbling track did elicit higher heart rate levels on the dribbling track than during small group play (**Figure 26**). Football specific exercise using dribbling or small group play may be performed as aerobic interval training. Heart rate monitoring during football specific exercise is a valid indicator of actual exercise intensity.

Figure 26. Correlation Between HR-VO2 Comparisons of SSGs and Dribbling Based on an Incremental Treadmill Test - A Linear Regression is Shown (from Hoff et al., 2002).

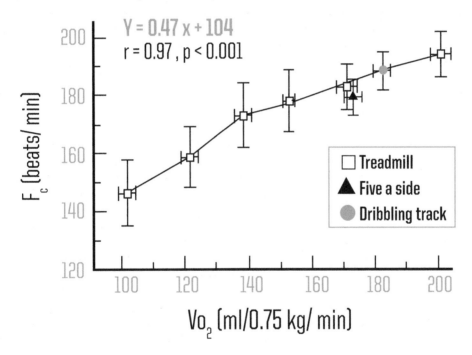

The Effect of Player Numbers

Recent research has indicated that high intensity efforts are increased when the player numbers are reduced (Platt et al, 2001; Jones and Drust, 2007). Conversely, this conclusion has been questioned by Owen et al (2013) as their recent findings show how less players per side within a functional *SSG* revealed a higher speed of play (metres per minute) when compared to medium and large sided games, but significantly less high intensity efforts. These findings concur to those professed by Hill-Haas et al (2008), who observed increased levels of maximal and average sprint duration and distance in accordance to increased player numbers.

It is of interest to note that the analysis of *SSGs*, *MSGs* and *LSGs* should be treated specifically with regard to speed thresholds. Indeed, it is much easier and probable for a player to attain a high speed threshold (i.e. 18 km/h) when playing on a large pitch compared to a smaller area e.g. playing 8 v 8 in a 65 x 50 yard area, compared to 3 v 3 in a 20 x 30 yard area. Analysis of the activity should therefore be done with respect to real internal load, largely influenced by

accelerations/decelerations and changes of direction, rather than just speed alone.

Time Spent at High Heart Rate (HR) Thresholds

Previous research by Stolen et al (2005) has shown that time spent at higher *HR* thresholds is vitally important for improving aerobic fitness in football players and that *HR* responses during match play range between 80 and 90% of the *HRmax*. According to the findings from Owen et al (2011) the comparisons for the 3 v 3 (+GKs) small sided game format resulted in significantly different amounts of time spent in the higher intensity *HR* zones (>85%*HRmax*). Specifically, during the *SSGs*, players spent significantly less time in the 71–84% *HRmax* zone and longer in the >85% *HRmax* zone, when compared to the *LSGs*.

In a similar study, Hill-Haas et al (2010) revealed how players following a generic training regime accumulated more time at reduced training intensity (<80 %*HRmax*), and less total training time at higher training intensities (>90 % *HRmax*) as shown in *Table 12* below (Hill-Haas et al, 2010).

Table 12. Comparison Between Times Spent Between Various HR Zone Thresholds Within a Generic Training Group (GTG) and a Small Sided Game Training Group (SSG) (from Hill-Haas et al., 2010).

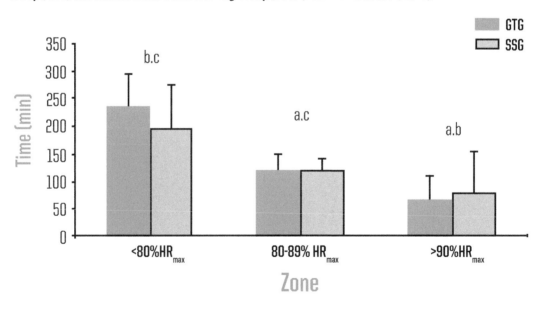

Small Sided Games vs. Traditional Fitness Methods

Although there has recently been increased support for the research into the use of *SSGs* as a football specific training approach, as opposed to traditional interval training (Little and Williams, 2006; Rampinini et al, 2007), an improved understanding of the reliability of the acute physiological and perceptual responses (*HR*, *bLa* and *RPE*) and performance is needed. One such study has recently attempted to examine the variability in the physiological, perceptual and movement profiles of various small sided games (2 v 2; 4 v 4; 6 v 6). According to Hill-Haas et al (2007) the study showed that various *SSGs* played (continuous or interval) would provide reliable internal and external loads, subsequently allowing coaches to maintain high levels of confidence in the method and provide an alternative to traditional running based interval training for developing and maintaining aerobic fitness. Additionally, due to the high reproducibility shown through data exposing the internal training load (*RPE* and *HR*) in conjunction with the external training load measures (*GPS* movement profiles), it was recommended that a higher priority should be placed on the player's heart rate (*HR*) and rate of perceived exertion (*RPE*) responses when monitoring football training.

Small sided games have been reported to increase players' motivation when compared to generic running intervals (Hill-Haas et al, 2009). These increased motivation levels maybe a result of using the ball and that they are more sport-specific in their approach to train the physical qualities needed to attain high levels of performance within competition. Consequently, these increased motivation levels may result in substantial increases in training intensity. Having described the physical demands associated with *SSGs* as a training regimen, the next progression surrounding the implementation is how to best implement *SSGs* in order to maximise the efficiency of the sessions and preparation of the players. Specific questions that may be asked are:

- How many players per game?

- What pitch size should we use?

- How many games should be used within a session?

- How long should the games be?

- How long should the recovery time between games be?

In an attempt to answer some of these specific questions, Hill-Haas et al., (2009) compared a 7 week football specific *SSG* programme and mixed generic fitness training on selected physiological, perceptual and performance variables. The details of the study were as follows:

- 25 elite youth players were randomly allocated to either a *SSG* or a *Generic Training (GTG)* group.

- Each group completed 2 fitness training sessions per week of equal duration and intensity.

- Prior to the start of the study, each player completed a *VO2max* treadmill test, *Multistage Fitness Test (MSFT)*, Yo-Yo Intermittent Recovery Test Level 1 (*YYIRTL1*), 12 × 20 metre test of Repeated Sprint Ability (*RSA*) and a 20 metre sprint test before and after training.

- Continued measurements of *HR*, *RPE* and perceptual fatigue measures were recorded throughout the training period.

The following conclusions were made from the study:

- No significant differences in training heart rate or perceptual well-being measures were found between the 2 groups, although the *GTG* did indicate their training intervention seemed substantially more intense than the *SSG* group.

- No changes found in either group for *VO2max*, *MSFT*, *RSA* or sprint performance but improvements were found in *YYIRTL1* performance for both groups during the study.

- Hill-Haas et al (2009) suggested that no changes between the groups were found regarding the *YYIRTL1* and highlighted how the results show both types of training are equally effective at improving pre-season football specific aerobic performance, even though the *GTG* was perceived to be of a higher intensity.

Football Conditioning: A Modern Scientific Approach

Table 13. *Summary of Small Sided Games Training Intervention* (from Hill-Haas et al., 2009).

WEEK	SESSION 1	REPS x DURATION / REST	PITCH SIZE	SESSION 2	REPS x DURATION / REST	PITCH SIZE	TOTAL DURATION
1	3v3	*3 x* 11min / 3min	30 x 20 m	7v7	*3 x* 13min / 2min	25 x 35 m	72 min
2	3v3	*4 x* 9min/2min	30 x 20 m	7v7	*3 x* 11min / 2min	55 x 40 m	69 min
3	3v3	*6 x* 6min / 1min	30 x 15 m	6v6	*3 x* 13min / 2min	40 x 30 m	75 min
4	6v6	*3 x* 11min / 2min	45 x 30 m	5v5 +1 / 5v6	*3 x* 11min / 2min	60 x 40 m	66 min
5	6v6 +1 / 6v7	*3 x* 13min / 2min	50 x 30 m	5v5	*3 x* 11min / 2min	45 x 35 m	72 min
6	6v6	*3 x* 10min / 2min	50 x 40 m	6v6	*3 x* 12min / 2min	40 x 30 m	66 min
7	2v2	*3 x* 7min / 1min	20 x 15 m	4v4	*2 x* 11min / 2min	40 x 20 m	43 min

Table 14. *Summary of Generic Training Intervention* (from Hill-Haas et al., 2009).

WEEK	SESSION 1: PRESCRIPTION (Repetitions x duration or distance/rest)	SESSION 2: PRESCRIPTION (Repetitions x duration or distance/rest)	DURATION (min)
1	**AP:** 10 x 30s/60s; 8 x 45s/90s	**RSA:** 7 x 34m/35s (1 set) **PH:** 3 x 5s/15s; 3 x 10s/20s; 3 x 15s/30s; 3 x 30s/60s; 3 x 45s/60s; 3 x 60s/90s; 3 x 90s/90s	70
2	**SL:** 15 min **SP:** S8 x 15m/15s; 8 x 20m/20s; 10 x 20m/40s; 4 x 15m/10s **CODS:** 8 min	**AP:** 8 x 60s/90s; 10 x 30s/45s	69
3	**RSA:** 7 x 34m/35s (1 set) **PIH:** 2 x 90s/90s; 2 x 60s/90s; 2 x 45s/60s; 4 x 30s/60s; 3 x 20s/40s; 4 x 15s/30s; 4 x 10s/20s; 4 x 5s/15s	**SL:** 15 min **SP:** 9 x 15m/15s; 9 x 20m/20s; 10 x 10m/40s; 5 x 15m/10s **CODS:** 10 min	75
4	**AP:** 10 x 8 x 60s/60s; 1 x 10 x 45s/45s	**RSA:** 7 x 34m/35s (1 set) **PH:** 3 x 5s/15s; 3 x 30s/60s; 4 x 20s/40s; 5 x 15s/30s; 5 x 10s/20s; 5 x 5s/15s; 1 x 45s/60s; 1 x 60s/90s; 1 x 90s/90s	66
5	**AP:** 1 x 11 x 30s/60s; 1 x 9 x 45s/90s	**SL:** 8 min **SP:** 10 x 10m/15s; 10 x 20m/20s; 10 x 10m/40s; 6 x 15m/10s **CODS:** 12 min	72
6	**RSA:** 7 x 34m/35s (1 set) **PIH:** 2 x 90s/90s; 2 x 60s/90s; 2 x 45s/60s; 4 x 30s/60s; 3 x 20s/40s; 4 x 15s/30s; 4 x 10s/20s; 4 x 5s/15s **RSA:** 7 x 34m/35s (1 set)	**AP:** 1 x 9 x 60s/90s; 1 x 11 x 30s/45s	66
7	**PIH:** 1 x 90s/90s; 1 x 60s/45s; 1 x 45s/60s; 3 x 30s/60s; 2 x 20s/40s; 3 x 15s/30s; 3 x 10s/20s; 3 x 5s/15s	**AP:** 1 x 6 x 30s/60s; 1 x 5 x 45s/90s	43

* The table represents the total training time of 2 conditioning sessions per week

AP = *Aerobic Power (intensity > 90% HRmax)*

PIH = *Prolonged Intermittent High Intensity Interval (maximum intensity)*

SP = *Sprint Training (10 m, 15 m and 20 m sprints)*

CODS = *Change of Direction Speed Drills*

RSA = *Repeated Sprint Ability (maximum intensity)*

SL = *Speed Ladder Drills*

Small Sided Games in Elite Football

To the author's knowledge, the recent study by Owen et al (2012) is the only investigation to date that has used a specific **SSG** game format amongst elite professional football players in an attempt to research the physiological performance benefits. Within the study, 3 v 3 + goalkeepers was the specific game format used which is suggested to be the most common type of **SSG** amongst published training interventions (Clemente et al, 2012), even though within the elite level of professional football training, 4 v 4 and 5 v 5 games are a more commonly used approach. The **SSGs** were played in a 25 x 30 yard area, which is 125m² per player and is suggested to be the approximate ratio within competitive matches. Owen et al (2012) used the **SSGs** training intervention (*Figure 27* below) with elite football players in the Scottish Premier League during a mid-season break. The intervention included players performing 7 sessions of the **SSG** format over a 4 week period. Each game lasted 3 minutes with a 2 minute passive recovery between games. Pre and post-testing sessions took place over a 2 day period:

- **Day 1:** Anthropometry and Repeated Sprint Ability (**RSA**) assessments

- **Day 2:** Treadmill based Running Economy (**CR**) and blood lactate (**bLa**) assessment.

The study concluded that the 4 week **SSG** training intervention resulted in significant improvements in **RSA**, indicated via improved 10 metre sprint times, total sprint times and significantly smaller percentage reductions in fatigue. Furthermore, the **SSGs** led to improvements in running economy (**CR**) revealed through significantly reduced **VO2** and heart rates at running speeds of 9, 11, and 14 km per hour.

Overall, the recent studies discussing the use of SSGs as a way of positively influencing players football performance capabilities, demonstrate that implementing a periodized SSG training intervention not only creates the same physical benefits of generic, non-football specific sessions (Hill-Haas et al, 2009) *but has the potential to significantly enhance physical profiles at the elite level* (Owen et al, 2012).

Conclusion

Being able to develop physical characteristics in conjunction to the technical and tactical elements of the game makes **SSGs** an appealing training methodology for fitness coaches, players, and technical coaches alike. Reducing the overall energy expended during a match through the development of running economy (**CR**) and improving players repeated sprint ability (**RSA**) through small sided games, opens up the current limited literature in this area for further research development as these are fundamental components determining player performance at the elite level. In addition, it may be realistic to suggest that **SSGs** may overload, and continually stress the body in order to increase the efficiency and subsequently improve a player's ability to recover from maximal exertions during the course of the game, shown through the improvement in **RSA**.

Figure 27. The Small Sided Game Training Structure Used Within the Study (by Owen et al., 2012).

	Monday	Tuesday	Wednesday	Thursday	Friday	Saturday	Sunday
Week 0				Pretest	Rest	Pretest	Day off
Week 1	Tech + Tact	SSGs 1 + IP	LITr	Tech + Tact	SSGs 2 +IP	LITr	Day off
Week 2	Tech + Tact	SSGs 3 + IP	LITr	Tech + Tact	SSGs 4 +IP	LITr	Day off
Week 3	Tech + Tact	SSGs 5 + IP	LITr	Tech + Tact	SSGs 6 +IP	LITr	Day off
Week 4	SSGs 7 + IP	Tech + Tact	LITr	Posttest	Rest	Posttest	Day off

IP = Injury prevention (low intensity work)
LITr = Low intensity recovery session

Tact = Tactical session (low intensity)
Tech = Technical session (low intensity)

2. VARIABLES AFFECTING SMALL SIDED GAME INTENSITY

PITCH AREA

Previous authors studying the effects of changing pitch dimensions have found no significant differences in the frequency of most technical actions such as passing, receiving, dribbling, or interceptions (Tessitore et al, 2006; Kelly and Drust, 2008). However, findings from 2 particular studies did reveal a higher number of shots and defensive actions such as blocks and tackles within smaller sized pitches (Kelly and Drust, 2008; Owen et al, 2004). These increased levels of defensive actions within smaller dimensions may be attributed to there being less space, causing a decreased area between opposition players when in possession, more physical contact and less passing options. Subsequently, the increased number of shots may be because the goals are closer in distance, leading the players to make more attempts at goal.

According to Casamichana and Castellano (2010) the regularity of increased behavioural responses was found in direct relationship with the reduction of playing area, which is consistent with previous literature in this area (Kelly and Drust, 2009; Owen et al, 2004; Tessitore et al, 2006). However, these earlier studies only reported a significant difference for tackling and shooting instances, whereas the study by Casamichana and Castellano (2010) found a significant difference in the number of interceptions, control and dribble, control and shoot and defensive clearances. Therefore, it would appear that the size of the pitch is of paramount importance when trying to expose or target certain individuals with more specific positional technical aspects.

Earlier research investigating the effects of changing pitch sizes seem to agree that changes to the dimensions of the playing areas have significant effects on both physical and technical demands imposed at various levels (Rampinini et al, 2007; Kelly and Drust, 2008; Owen et al, 2004; Tessitore et al, 2006). It is important coaches try to standardise playing areas and player numbers, or risk the chance of producing a very different physical and technical outcome from similar training contents.

Further research surrounding the effects of pitch size on performance is needed at the elite level of football. Recent research has also agreed standardisation of pitch size in order to examine the effects of changing pitch sizes on physiological outcomes further. Aguiar et al (2012) has suggested that the origin of the disagreement between authors is based on the fact that research has been performed using several different pitch sizes.

In addition to previous statements, observations from recent publications regarding the influence on the technical output of specific sessions found no significant differences in the frequency of most actions, such as passing, receiving, dribbling, interceptions etc (Kelly and Drust, 2008; Tessitore et al., 2006). However, other examinations of the technical analysis within *SSGs* revealed higher numbers of shots and tackles within smaller sized pitch areas (Kelly and Drust, 2008; Owen et al., 2004).

Figure 28. Frequency of Defensive Skills Within Various SSGs Irrespective of Pitch Size (Owen et al., 2004).

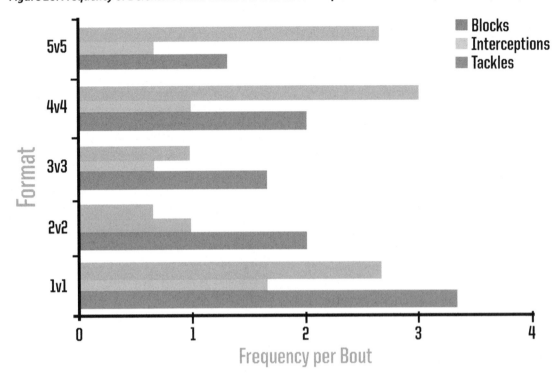

Table 15. Characteristics of 3 Small Sided Game (5 v 5 + GKs) Training Formats (Casamichana and Castellano, 2010).
SSG L = Large pitch size; SSG M = Medium pitch size; SSG s = Small pitch size

VARIABLES	CM FORMAT STANDARD PITCH	SMALL SIDED GAME FORMAT		
		SSG L	SSG M	SSG s
Duration	2 x 40 min	8 min	8 min	8 min
Pitch Size	88 x 62 m	62 x 44 m	50 x 35 m	32 x 23 m
Playing Area	5456 m²	2728 m²	1750 m²	736 m²
Grid Ratio (Length to Width)	1 ; 4 ; 1	1 ; 4 ; 1	1 ; 4 ; 1	1 ; 4 ; 1
Ratio per player	272.8 m²	272.8 m²	175 m²	73.6 m²
Goalkeepers	Yes	Yes	Yes	Yes
Rules	Same as 11v11	_	No Offsides	_
Coach encouragement	Yes	Yes	Yes	Yes

Football Conditioning: A Modern Scientific Approach

Table 16. Table to Show the Technical Demands of Changing Pitch Dimensions
(from Casamichana and Castellano, 2010).

Average (+ standard deviations) for the Observed Behaviours of Players in the Different Small Sided Game Formats.

*The final column shows the correlations between **Effective Playing Time (EPT)** and each of the physical variables*

ACTION	SSG L	SSG M	SSG S	CORRELATION WITH EPT
Tackle	3.0 ± 0.9 (2.1 to 3.9)	4.5 ± 2.1 (2.3 to 6.7)	3.0 ± 2.7 (0.2 to 5.8)	0.148
Interception	6.3 ± 1.5 (4.7 to 7.9)	8.3 ± 2.6 (5.6 to 11.0)	11.2 ± 3.1 (7.9 to 14.4) [a]	-0.522 *
Control	1.7 ± 1.7 (-0.2 to 3.5)	1.8 ± 1.3 (0.4 to 3.2)	2.8 ± 0.9 (1.8 to 3.9)	-0.394
Control and Dribble	1.7 ± 0.8 (0.8 to 2.5)	4.5 ± 1.5 (2.9 to 6.1) [c]	5.2 ± 1.7 (3.4 to 7.0) [a]	-0.494 *
Control, Dribble & Pass	14.2 ± 4.2 (0.8 to 18.5)	13.8 ± 5.5 (8.1 to 19.6)	10.2 ± 6.5 (3.3 to 17.0)	-0.277
Control and Pass	18.7 ± 4.3 (14.1 to 23.2)	16.8 ± 6.1 (10.4 to 23.2)	14.5 ± 6.6 (7.6 to 21.4)	-0.204
Control and Shoot	2.2 ± 1.7 (0.4 to 3.9)	1.8 ± 1.6 (0.1 to 3.5)	5.0 ± 2.4 (2.5 to 7.5) [b]	-0.451
Control, Dribble & Shoot	1.0 ± 0.6 (0.3 to 1.7)	1.5 ± 1.97 (-0.6 to 3.6)	2.5 ± 0.5 (1.9 to 3.1)	-0.346
Header	1.7 ± 1.0 (0.6 to 2.7)	2.3 ± 2.2 (-0.3 to 4.7)	4.0 ± 2.1 (1.8 to 6.2)	-0.542
First Touch Pass	9.0 ± 5.6 (3.1 to 14.9)	11.3 ± 2.9 (8.2 to 14.4)	10.3 ± 3.3 (6.8 to 13.8)	-0.105
Clearance	2.3 ± 1.0 (1.2 to 3.4)	3.8 ± 2.6 (1.1 to 6.6)	8.0 ± 2.9 (4.9 to 11.1) [ab]	-0.566
Putting Ball in Play	12.2 ± 4.3 (7.6 to 16.7)	16.5 ± 1.6 (14.8 to 18.2)	27.7 ± 3.8 (23.6 to 31.7) [ab]	-0.871 **

*SSG L = Large pitch size; **SSG M** = Medium pitch size; **SSG S** = Small pitch size*

Table 17. Pitch Area (m²) Used Within Recent Small Sided Game Research (adapted from Aguiar et al., 2012).

SSG FORMAT	PITCH SIZE USED			REFERENCE
	MIN		MAX	
1 v 1		100m² (50m²/P)		Dellal et al (2008)
2 v 2	400m² (100m²/P)		800m² (200m²/P)	Dellal et al (2008); Hill-Haas et al (2009)
3 v 3	240m2 (40m²/P)		2500m² (416.6m²/P)	Owen et al (2004)
4 v 4	240m² (30m²/P)		2208m² (276m²/P)	Owen et al (2012); Owen et al (2011); Coutts et al (2009)
5 v 5	240m² (24m²/P)		2500m² (250m²/P)	Owen et al (2013); Owen et al (2004); Coutts et al (2009)
6 v 6	240m² (20m²/P)		2400m² (200m²/P)	Coutts et al (2009)
7 v 7	875m² (62.5m²/P)		2200m² (157.1m²/P)	Owen et al (2013); Coutts et al (2009)
8 v 8	2400m² (150m²/P)		2700m² (168.7m²/P)	Jones and Drust (2007); Dellal et al (2008)

Football Conditioning: A Modern Scientific Approach

Figure 29. Comparison of Skills Within Various Small Sided Games Irrespective of Pitch Sizes
(from Owen et al., 2004).

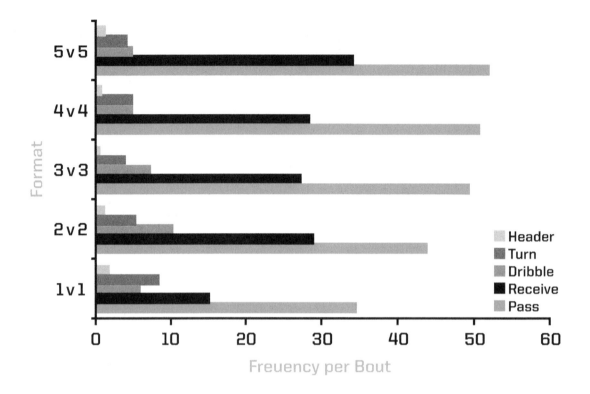

PLAYER NUMBERS

Modern literature surrounding the varying of player numbers within the same training area has been developed. Generally, it can be concluded that within **SSG** investigations, games with less players create a significantly increased heart rate (**HR**) response when compared to **LSGs** (Owen et al, 2011; Hill-Haas et al, 2010; Little and Williams, 2006; Owen et al, 2013). Although some reports have shown contrasting conclusions due to the lack of significance between games with respect to the **HR** assessments (Dellal et al, 2008; Hill-Haas et al, 2008), the consensus tends to promote the theory that different game formats (e.g. 2 v 2; 3 v 3) in the same area may create different physiological and movement characteristics (Williams and Owen et al, 2007; Hill-Haas et al, 2010; Katis and Kellis, 2009; Owen et al, 2004; Rampinini et al, 2007). The increased physiological response (**HR** and **bLa** values) to **SSGs** with less players may be significantly related to the increased technical demand in limited space and the reduced number of players involved within training sessions also leads to an increased technical exposure for each player (Owen et al, 2004). According to Dellal et al (2011) the number of ball touches is considered to be a fundamental factor in elite professional football. Exposing players to more technical actions throughout the course of a training session will therefore lead to improvements in performance.

The Effect on Number of Passes

These previous studies have only examined the influence of altering the player numbers with teams maintaining a numerical equality (e.g. 2 v 2 or 4 v 4). It should be noted that there are a few studies concerning the technical demands imposed upon elite level professional football players through the use of **SSG** training interventions (Dellal et al., 2011; Dellal et al., 2012) compared to **MSGs** and **LSGs**. It has been concluded that there are significant differences between each game type (**SSGs**, **MSGs**, **LSGs**) with respect to number of passes, as shown in **Table 18**

on the next page (Owen et al, 2013). The results have shown that the greater number of players on the pitch (e.g. 9 v 9; 10 v 10 and 11 v 11), the less number of total passes will be made. This may be because a reduced number of players on a smaller pitch leads to more pressure applied on the person in possession of the ball, which subsequently increases the need to pass. Large sided games do not expose players to as much pressure when in possession, therefore allowing slightly more time on the ball.

The Effect on Number of Dribbles

Furthermore, there were significantly more dribbles within the **SSGs** compared to **MSGs** and **LSGs** (**Table 18** on the next page) in the study by Owen et al (2013). Due to there being less passing options within the **SSGs**, the increased need for players to dribble past opponents to create space to maintain possession is a key component. However, it has been suggested from the limited papers in this area that the number of players should be carefully considered by coaches in their organization, with a periodized approach to weekly training structures. It seems consenting that games with small numbers of players can deliver a more effective technical training stimulus, due to the overload in technical actions being increased in accordance to the decrease in player numbers (Owen et al, 2013; Jones and Drust, 2007; Katis and Kellis, 2009; Owen et al, 2004).

Periodized Training

Determining which sided games to use on specific training days in order to achieve a specific training adaptation from both a technical and physical perspective is a fundamental part of the training design process. Part of this training design action will generally involve coaches selecting fixed and equal team numbers. Recently though, Aguiar et al, (2012) has suggested that it is becoming more common practice for coaches to use **SSG** formats involving

a team playing with a fixed numerical advantage versus teams with a numerical disadvantage. One of the limited studies published regarding the overload (numerical advantage) vs. underload (numerical disadvantage) teams concluded that, despite fixed underload teams recording a significantly higher rate of perceived exertion (*RPE*) compared with the fixed overload teams, there were no differences in movement characteristics and physiological responses (Hill-Haas et al, 2010). According to these authors, the overload/underload situations may provide a useful variation in *SSG* intensity or act as a technical/tactical training method for the development of defensive and attacking plays. However, the possibility of these

different overload vs. underload formats revealing significantly different technical responses in order to achieve a specific outcome needs to be confirmed through additional research.

Further research investigating the development of specific technical/tactical modifications within professional football at the elite level, such as whether to include the offside rule or not, limiting player movements within certain positional areas, would certainly be of great interest to assist in the development of a technical, tactical AND physical periodization structure.

Table 18. Comparison of Technical Performance Between Small Sided Games, Medium Sided Games and Large Sided Games (from Owen et al., 2013).

*SSG = 4 v 4; MSG = 5 v 5 to 8 v 8; LSG = 9 v 9 to 11 v 11.

ACTION	SSG [a]	MSG [b]	LSG [c]	EFFECT SIZE
Pass	184.8 (16.8) [bc]	147.5 (20.6) [c]	121.2 (5.0)	SSG vs MSG: 1.5 SSG vs LSG: 3.7 MSG v LSG: 1.3
Receive	147.8 (23.3) [bc]	117.2 (20.0)	94.0 (2.1)	SSG vs MSG: 1.0 SSG vs LSG: 2.3 MSG v LSG: 1.2
Turn	29.0 (2.4)	31.2 (3.1)	29.0 (5.8)	SSG vs MSG: 0.6 SSG vs LSG: 0 MSG v LSG: 0.3
Dribble	27.0 (4.9) [bc]	14.3 (7.3)	16.7 (3.5)	SSG vs MSG: 1.5 SSG vs LSG: 1.8 MSG v LSG: 0.3
Header	3.3 (2.2) [c]	3.7 (1.4) [c]	9.2 (2.2)	SSG vs MSG: 0.2 SSG vs LSG: 2.0 MSG v LSG: 2.2
Tackle	14.8 (4.8)	9.0 (3.6)	10.3 (1.5)	SSG vs MSG: 1.0 SSG vs LSG: 0.9 MSG v LSG: 0.3
Block	6.3 (3.1)	7.8 (1.6)	9.3 (2.1)	SSG vs MSG: 0.4 SSG vs LSG: 0.8 MSG v LSG: 0.6
Interception	14.5 (8.2)	18.5 (2.1)	23.7 (6.7)	SSG vs MSG: 0.5 SSG vs LSG: 0.9 MSG v LSG: 0.8
Shot	52.0 (7.4) [bc]	3.3 (2.2) [c]	12.8 (6.3)	SSG vs MSG: 1.8 SSG vs LSG: 4.2 MSG v LSG: 1.8

* *a, b, c in table show a significant difference between the different game types - SSG (a), MSG (b), and LSG (c).*

E.g. In the SSG pass column, 184.8 has 'b,c' next to the value because there is a significant difference in that number when compared with MSGs (b) and LSGs (c).

CONCURRENT EFFECTS OF PITCH AREA AND PLAYER NUMBERS

Previous research within this area has shown *SSGs* (3 v 3) to create higher heart rate (*HR*) responses and number of ball touches per player, but fewer total ball touches per game when compared to *LSGs* (Owen et al, 2011). Unfortunately, this particular study only accounted for *HR* and technical parameters and did not detail activity profiles (movement analysis). Similarly, Dellal et al (2012) found all positional roles presented higher *HR* values and greater high-intensity activities during *SSGs* (4 v 4) but with lower blood lactate concentrations when compared to *LSGs* (actual match play), although we have already questioned the non-reliable data regarding the use of *bLa* as a match intensity predictor previously.

Despite the extensive research into the physical, technical and movement profiles of *SSGs* (4 v 4, 5 v 5) and their use within football (Owen et al, 2011; Dellal et al, 2011; Casamichana and Castellano, 2010; Casamichana et al, 2012; Owen et al, 2012), our understanding of how to maximise their function is not complete. Previous research has discussed the physiological responses of small sided games in isolation, however, the implementation of these games should be carefully considered as part of an advanced planning structure (Owen et al, 2012) which may be more representative of the day to day activities within a professional football club. In order to make effective use of *SSGs* as a conditioning stimulus, a comprehensive understanding of the associated physiological and movement responses needs to be developed for all sided-game variations (Hill-Hass et al, 2009).

Owen et al (2011) indicated that when concurrently increasing pitch sizes and player numbers, a large practical difference between small and large sided games in terms of the technical demands is seen (e.g. less number of blocks, headers, interceptions, passes and more dribbles, shots, and tackles). In conjunction with these findings, *SSGs* induce significantly less total ball touches per game, but significantly greater ball touches per individual when compared to *LSGs*.

The different technical demands imposed upon players when varying pitch size and player numbers highlights how coaches are able to provide more position specific training through the use of specific sided training game formats. For example, specific *SSGs* may be better suited for the technical demands of midfield or forward players as they create more opportunities to dribble, tackle and shoot in accordance to the increased touches and/or involvement with the ball. Opposing this, it may be more appropriate for defenders to develop technically and tactically with *LSGs* based on the research suggesting these game types give players more opportunity to block, intercept and perform aerial challenges.

These suggestions are in agreement with another study comparing the differences of medium sized games (8 v 8) and *SSGs* (4 v 4) (Jones and Drust, 2007). This particular investigation revealed significant technical differences with respect to the number of ball touches. The authors highlighted that the number of ball touches increased within the *SSGs* when there were less players.

Overall, it may be concluded that the concurrent changes of pitch size and player numbers leads to significant changes in technical demands imposed upon players. It may be suggested that the tactical requirements placed on players as the player numbers increase within the session, becomes greater. For example, the medium sided games and large sided games may subconsciously see players reverting to specific tactical positions, with small sided games having the opposite effect, resulting in players pressing the opposition and rotating more through a limited tactical approach. This subsequently increases the intensity of play, as shown through an increased internal load (*HR* responses) and external load (metres per minute).

RULE CHANGES

Recent literature has discussed many ways of manipulating the intensity and technical load of football training games. One of these suggestions, apart from the player numbers and pitch size, is through influencing or imposing technical rule restrictions on the players (Aguiar et al, 2012; Clemente et al, 2012). According to some researchers, coaches could increase the total distance covered in sprinting and in high-intensity running, provide more opportunities for 1 v 1 duels, increase the amount of ball touches/possessions, as well as expose their players to more demanding game-related situations.

From the current literature, it seems that influencing or changing the technical rule aspects of various sided training games can significantly impact on the physiological and movement response demands imposed upon the players. It should be noted however, that further investigations are needed in order to quantify the exact effect specific rule changes may induce to position specific movements and demands, as to date, the study by Dellal et al (2011) is the only investigation involving the use of rule changes at the elite level. There seems to be a huge void within the literature examining the influence of modifying the number of ball touches allowed per player, with respect to the physical and technical responses at the elite level. The limited research studies performed in this area have been performed with either youth players (Sampaio et al, 2007) or amateur players (Aroso et al, 2004) and revealed increases in *RPE* values and *bLa* levels when *SSGs* were played without rules vs. maximum of 2 or 3 touches. In both studies however, it should be noted that no changes in the percentage of *HRmax* were found. Additional research similar to Dellal et al (2011) involving further technical modifications utilised within professional football at the elite level, such as varying the number of ball touches per player, inclusion of the offside rule or not, limitations of player movement to highlight a specific tactical element are needed.

Recently, Ngo et al, (2012) examined the effect of manipulating defensive rules within *SSGs*. The study involved the comparison analysis of 3 v 3 games with and without man-marking on exercise intensity. It was revealed from the findings that amongst youth football players there was a 4.5% increase in *HR* response when implementing the man-marking rule in the *SSG*, therefore highlighting the fact that the intensity of a *SSG* can be significantly increased when using man-marking tactics.

Throughout various levels of the game, technical coaches may often modify the playing rules to achieve higher exercise intensity, induce a greater technical demand or attempt to improve tactical skills. Confidence in implementing such changes for a desired outcome has been reassured through research (Dellal et al 2008) suggesting that rule changes within training may provide an opportunity to influence or further stress the physical and technical demands. To be successful within the modern game, elite professional football players are required to play the game at an extremely high intensity, with fewer ball touches in order to maintain possession within their team (Dellal, 2008).

One particular study within this area has recently been performed, highlighting some very interesting findings (Dellal et al, 2011). The players performed 3 different *SSG* formats (2 v. 2; 3 v 3; 4 v 4) on 3 different occasions in which the number of ball touches was fixed pre-game to either 1 touch , 2 touch and unlimited amount of touches (free play). The physical (*HR, bLa* and *RPE*) and technical demands were analysed with the following results:

- **Technical:** The percentage of successful passes and number of duels (1 v 1 situations) were significantly lower when the *SSG* was played with 1 touch.

- **Physical:** *SSGs* played with 1 touch rule led to increases in *bLa* concentration, RPE, movement demands (TDC), sprinting and *HI* running.

Study Conclusion

The authors of this investigation concluded that by altering the number of ball touches allowed in specific sided training games, the technical and physical demands can be significantly manipulated, highlighting the fact that coaches should carefully implement game rules (e.g. 1 touch, 2 touch or free play) in order to achieve a specific purpose from sessions (Dellal et al, 2011).

Table 19. Technical Responses Within Different SSG Formats Involving Different Rule Changes (from Dellal et al., 2011). *(TOTALS ARE AVERAGES)*

FORMAT	RULES	NUMBER OF DUELS	DUELS PER MINUTE	SUCCESSFUL PASSES (%)	NUMBER OF BALL LOSSES	BALL LOSSES PER MINUTE	TOTAL NUMBER OF POSSESSIONS
2 v 2	**1 Touch**	17.1	2.1	42.5	23.5	2.9	50.6
	2 Touch	28.5	3.6	60.5	14.1	1.8	41.4
	Free Play	26.1	3.2	66.4	13.9	1.7	40.9
3 v 3	**1 Touch**	30.9	2.5	52	17.1	1.4	51.8
	2 Touch	28.1	2.4^	69.9	15.1	1.3	43.7
	Free Play	26.8	2.2	71	14.3	1.2	41.7
4 v 4	**1 Touch**	18.0	1.1	49.8	14.8	0.9	41.6
	2 Touch	16.5	1.0	68.9	13.6	0.8	34.7
	Free Play	25.1	1.5	73.4	13.2	0.8	31.5

Football Conditioning: A Modern Scientific Approach

(a) Varying Game Performance Outcomes

Within many levels of football training (i.e. youth to elite professional level), coaches use many different methods of scoring. One of the most used methods in order to vary training sessions is through the use of goals. According to previous research one of the less published or described methods of affecting playing intensity is through the method of scoring (Bangsbo, 1994; Balsom, 2000; Mallo and Navarro, 2008) or providing an aim or target of the game (e.g. scoring goals or maintaining possession for a set number of passes). Even though the main aim of the game is to score more goals than the opposition, according to Clemente et al (2012) no specific research into the effects of scoring methods involving goals (small or traditional sized) on the technical or physical demands within football have been published.

It may be suggested that the use of smaller goals instead of traditional sized goals may limit a player's goal scoring opportunities due to a significantly reduced target. Based on this notion, the players may then need to recycle possession to create a better goal scoring opportunity, therefore maintaining possession

for a longer period of time, which subsequently leads to increased intensity and movement profiles.

A recent study investigating the manipulation of 3 specific target conditions has been reported. Duarte et al (2010) assessed the outcome of 3 specific conditions within their study:

- **A) The Line Goal**, which meant the players needed to score by dribbling over an extended line at the end of the pitch .

- **B) The Double Goal**, which gave the players a chance of scoring in either of 2 goals situated at opposite ends of the pitch.

- **C) The Traditional Central Goal**, with the aim of scoring as within a normal game in only one goal.

Results from the study highlighted how heart rate (*HR*) responses associated with the line goal task (A) constraint is lower than that associated with both the double goal (B) and central goal constraints (C) (Duarte et al, 2010). Therefore, according to authors, these effects represent a more cardiovascular standardised stimulation of the players involved in the line goal task.

Figure 30 A. Example of Game Modifications - 'The Line Goal' (described in Duarte et al., 2010).

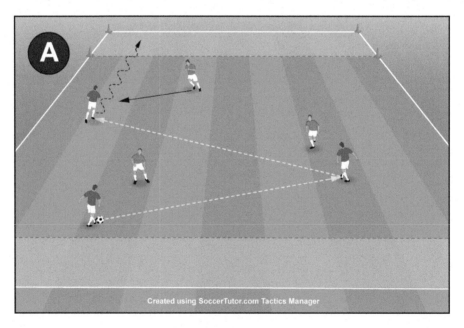

*Figure 30 B. Example of Game Modifications - **'The Double Goal'*** (described in Duarte et al., 2010).

*Figure 30 C. Example of Game Modifications - **'The Traditional Central Goal'*** (described in Duarte et al., 2010).

(b) Collective Possession
(With vs. Without direction)

In contrast to training games that include a scoring opportunity (line goal, 2 goals, 1 goal) there are many coaches who perform specific sessions without the aid of a particular target. However, playing possession games without having to attack or defend a particular target such as goals or zones is not really specific to the competitive nature of the game, as there should always be an outcome of a training session.

There is a significant lack of research within the area surrounding the technical and physical comparisons of possession games vs. directional games (Aguiar et al, 2012; Clemente et al, 2012). At the elite level, many coaches have described the importance of the transition phases between attacking play, defensive play and vice versa, based on the fact that a high proportion of goals are scored in this way. In fact, FIFA's 2006 trend analysis of the modern game revealed that 70% of goals scored are done so within counter-attacking situations (less than 10 seconds) following a possession transition.

"...The most important thing in today's game is when the ball is won or lost..." (Gerard Houllier)

If players are not faced with any tactical limitations within the game and are not maintaining possession in order to build toward a specific target or goal scoring direction, then it may be suggested that a lower technical demand may be shown, however further research is needed in order to justify these claims fully.

These suggestions of reduced intensity and subsequent technical demands due to no specific directional element, may be based on similar findings from Mallo and Navarro (2008) who revealed analysis of the technical parameters according to the presence of goalkeepers. They found that there were a lower number of total technical actions in these situations (Mallo and Navarro, 2008).

The comparisons between including goalkeepers or not are discussed in more detail on the following page (part d).

(c) Coach Encouragement

It has been suggested that direct supervision and verbal encouragement whilst coaching football related exercises is shown to improve adherence to an exercise programme, increase training intensity and increase performance measures in a variety of training modes (Hill-Haas et al., 2011; Mazzetti et al, 2000).

The effect of coach encouragement is believed to be a fundamental variable in being able to significantly influence the physiological and subsequent technical stresses referred by many authors as one of the factors that influence the player's physiological response to *SSGs* (Aguiar et al, 2012; Clemente et al, 2012; Rampinini et al, 2007). This specific verbal encouragement provided by technical and conditioning related staff members is suggested to directly influence the physical exertion of the players, which may then add an additional technical demand as a result (Rampinini et al, 2007). These effects may play a fundamental role in the application of players within training because the external motivation provided by coach supervision can achieve greater physiological gains (Coutts et al, 2004).

As discussed, there has been a gradual increase within the literature regarding the effects of coach encouragement and its influence on the player's physiological response within various *SSGs* (Hill-Haas et al, 2011; Rampinini et al, 2007), however the technical responses of the inclusion of this method are still lacking in research. Of the literature researching the physical benefits of encouragement within football, Rampinini et al (2007) revealed increased *HR* response, *bLa* and *RPE* within *SSGs* when the addition of coach encouragement was used, in comparison to a game that included no encouragement. Subsequently, according to Hill-Haas et al, (2011) this variable can play a vital role within the implementation of *SSGs* as a training intervention, especially if the coaches involved consistently provide verbal encouragement throughout the working duration, when high intensity outcomes are planned or required within the session.

(d) Inclusion of Goalkeepers

The inclusion of goalkeepers within football specific training drills or **SSGs** is fundamental to the training of both the outfield players and the goalkeepers' specific development. Mallo and Navarro (2008) indicated that the inclusion of a goalkeepers significantly influenced the physiological and tactical elements of the players within the sessions. There was a suggestion that the inclusion of the goalkeepers within a sided-game format leads to a decreased intensity of play (Mallo and Navarro, 2008), however this factor would be dependent on the specific rules, an the tactical or technical focus of the session in comparison to other game rules or formats used. This suggestion was also confirmed by Dellal et al (2008) who concluded that a lower game intensity was found when the goalkeepers were present. It was found that lower **HR** responses were found within the game including goalkeepers, when compared to without them. These lower training intensities may not only be related to the inclusion of the goalkeepers, but potentially due to the specific directional nature of the play (e.g. working towards a goal). In accordance to this, any other directional specific sided game without the inclusion of the goalkeepers may result in a reduced training intensity as well (Aguiar et al, 2012; Clemente et al, 2012).

The technical effect of **SSGs** including goalkeepers versus no goalkeepers is a subject that requires further research due to the limited amount currently available. The physical differences have been reported to a more significant level than the technical element of the games. However, analysis of the technical parameters when goalkeepers are present has revealed a lower number of total technical actions (Mallo and Navarro, 2008).

Mallo and Navarro (2008) reported that the involvement of a goalkeeper within **SSGs** could potentially change the intensity related responses of the game as well as the tactical perspective due to the fact that some players may show increased levels of motivation than others, as they have the opportunity to shoot and score (Dellal et al, 2008). Furthermore, previous research suggests that the aim of trying to score and simultaneously protect their own goal from the opposition may have significantly influenced and led to greater player activity and subsequent exertion (Dellal et al, 2008; Stolen et al, 2005). From a defensive perspective, the inclusion of goalkeepers will probably lead to a more organised defensive structure in order to protect their goal, which may have played a fundamental part in the playing intensity.

Mallo and Navarro, (2008) reported significant decreases in %**HRmax**, total distance covered (**TDC**) and high intensity running during 3 v 3 small sided games including goalkeepers. The findings of this study also suggested that the reduced physiological and movement response of the games were due to the increased defensive organisation which subsequently reduced the intensity of play and the physiological and movement responses.

Recent research has however shown a contrasting opinion to Mallo and Navarro's findings as it was reported that a 12% increase was found amongst **HR** responses during 8 v 8 **SSGs** including goalkeepers (Dellal et al, 2011). The presence of goalkeepers may have increased motivation to both attack and defend, thereby increasing the physiological load (Dellal et al, 2011).

Currently, the influence goalkeepers have on the exercise intensity in **SSGs** within a football training environment is unclear, however, they may play an important role in maintaining the team structure and formation, as well as developing lines of communication within the training environment. These fundamental principles may then also significantly influence movement, skill and the physiological demand imposed upon players within the games. However, in order to gain clarity regarding the changes from a physical, technical and tactical perspective with the presence of goalkeepers, future studies are required to determine their influence.

Football Conditioning: A Modern Scientific Approach

(e) Duration and Number of Bouts

It has been well discussed that interval training through the use of **SSGs** is an efficient and effective way of promoting aerobic fitness and football-specific endurance developments (Owen et al, 2012), and that the use of this specific methodology to overload the competitive demands of the sport has attracted the interest of football related research (Dellal et al, 2011; Owen et al, 2011; Hill-Haas et al, 2011). Due to the fact that training adaptations are created through sport specific physical and technical stressors within the **SSGs**, ensuring adequate exercise intensity applied is arguably one of the key variables influencing the training response (McMillan et al, 2004). Having previously described the variables associated with ensuring a manipulation of intensity (player numbers, pitch sizes, coach encouragement etc) within **SSGs** (Owen et al, 2004; Dellal et al, 2008; Hill-Haas et al, 2011), a further factor that plays a significant role is bout duration. According to Franchini et al (2010), although bout duration plays a major part in the intensity of exercise, it seems to have been overlooked as a research topic.

To examine whether the increase in bout duration would affect the exercise intensity and technical actions, Franchini et al (2010) manipulated the training interval bout durations within a **SSG** format. It was concluded during the study that the increase in bout duration from 2 to 6 minutes resulted in a decrease in intensity between the 4th and 6th minute. Furthermore, the duration did not significantly influence the technical actions involved within the **SSG** or the **HR** changes (89.5% vs. 87.8% **HRmax**) and was suggested as not being sufficient enough to cause any different training adaptations or performance developments. Overall, Franchini et al (2010) concluded that coaches may use different bout durations to induce similar training intensities without compromising the technical proficiency of the players.

Although Franchini et al (2010) suggests that bout durations from 2 to 6 minutes within **SSGs** induce similar intensities of play from a **HR** perspective, according to Hoff et al (2002), pilot studies involving **SSGs** indicated that it would be necessary to use 4

minute periods of play to reach at least 3 minutes at high intensity. This is quite an important factor when deciding upon the duration of training interval bouts for athletic development, especially within **SSGs**, as there seems to be a direct relationship between training time at a high cardiovascular intensity and performance gains (Hoff et al, 2002; McMillan et al, 2004). Additionally, to ensure players reach and sustain the required intensity within **SSGs**, the bout duration must be long enough to cause an overload to allow for physiological adaptations to take place, without causing injury through fatigue. As Hoff et al (2002) suggested it takes approximately 1 minute for the **HR** to reach the required high intensity zone to cause performance gains, therefore suggesting that 2 minute bouts as used within the Franchini et al (2010) study may not be sufficient enough.

Choosing the correct bout durations when using **SSGs** as part of the training structure is very important to limit the risk of injury when in a fatigued state. **SSGs** involve accelerating, deceleration, twisting and turning, so the loadings placed upon the players within these game types could potentially be very high. Intermittent training bouts in the form of **SSGs** with changes of direction, physical contact, tackles, interceptions and blocks are physically demanding and extensive durations may lead to greater fatigue levels during **SSGs** as opposed to the shorter intensive durations. Repetitive games of shorter periods (3 to 4 minutes) following a shorter recovery may be more suited to **SSG** formats (Fox and Mathews, 1974).

Further research is needed regarding the work to rest ratio (W:R) periods used within **SSGs** as the key is to ensure sessions are efficient and allow for performance developments without risking injury. When discussing exercise bouts within training structures, Noakes, (2004) has suggested that it is vitally important to fully understand how the body reacts to the total duration of the exercise bout to be performed. It is also important how the individual's perception of effort is increased in order to prevent causing large amounts of muscle damage.

PHYSIOLOGY OF SMALL SIDED GAMES TRAINING IN FOOTBALL

By Hill-Haas, Dawson, Impellizeri & Coutts Sports Medicine 2011

Small sided games (SSGs) are played on reduced pitch areas, often using modified rules and involving a smaller number of players than traditional football. These games are less structured than traditional fitness training methods but are very popular training drills for players of all ages and levels.

ADJUSTABLE VARIABLES

Many prescriptive variables controlled by the coach can influence the exercise intensity during SSGs

PITCH AREA

COACH ENCOURAGEMENT

TRAINING METHOD
Continuous vs Interval

PLAYER NUMBERS

RULES

USE OF GOALKEEPER

KEY POINTS

1 In general, it appears that SSG exercise intensity is increased with the concurrent reduction in player numbers and increase in relative pitch area per player

2 However, the inverse relationship between the number of players in each SSG and exercise intensity does not apply to the time-motion characteristics.

3 Consistent coach encouragement can also increase training intensity, but most rule changes do not appear to strongly affect exercise intensity

4 SSGs containing fewer players can far exceed match intensity and elicit similar intensities to both long and short duration high intensity interval running

5 Fitness and football specific performance can be improved equally with SSGs and generic training drills

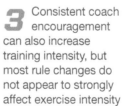

Designed by @YLMSportScience

3. PERIODIZATION OF SMALL SIDED GAMES

PERIODIZATION OF SMALL SIDED GAMES

As we well know from the literature surrounding sided games, many variables can be manipulated to significantly influence the intensity and speed of play. In order to maximise the weekly training structure within football it is imperative that players experience various levels of intensity and speed of movements in order to prepare for the competitive demands of match play. Periodization and its capacity to plan and design a schedule with the appropriate training load (intensity, volume, and frequency) play a key factor when attempting to avoid injury and enhance physical and technical performance. In this context, the term *'advanced planning'* or *'periodization'* should be considered as a functional strategy for the development of both performance and injury prevention. Arguably, this strategy of 'advanced planning' may be the most important factor influencing performance and injury prevention due to the fact that the technical staff implement and dictate most of the pitch based training sessions (Dellal et al, 2013). Advanced planning between technical, conditioning and medical staff is vital in order to elicit the correct volume, duration, and intensity of training and ensure maximum player freshness pre-game (Owen et al, 2013). Arguably, the limited publications available surrounding this topic is due to the fact that this particular area within the training design is coach dependant and more often than not led by the technical department.

Examining this topic further and based on the limited amount of research within this area related to *SSGs*, Owen et al (2012) investigated the effects of a periodized *SSG* training plan during a 4 week in-season break on the physical performance changes (i.e. speed, aerobic performance, and repeated sprint ability - *RSA*) within elite European football players. Elite male professional players who were competing in the UEFA Champions League at the time, participated in 7 separate *SSG* sessions (3 v 3 + goalkeepers). Each game lasted 3 minutes and the selected number of games (range from 5 to 11) increased over the

intervention period. The results from the *SSGs* intervention revealed the following:

- A significant improvement in repeated sprint ability (*RSA*) indicated by faster 10 metre sprint times and total sprint time duration.

- A smaller percentage reduction score for aerobic performance.

- An improvement in running economy (*CR*) shown through significantly reduced *VO2* and *HR* levels at running speeds of 9, 11 and 14 km per hour.

Owen et al (2012) concluded how the study demonstrated that implementing a periodized *SSG* training intervention during the 4 week in-season break is capable of improving elite professional football players' physical fitness characteristics. Therefore, it should be highlighted that being able to develop physical characteristics in conjunction to the technical and tactical elements of the game within a relatively short period of time, makes small sided games an appealing proposition for players and coaches alike, in their aim of developing physical profiles and subsequent performance.

4. WORKLOAD EVALUATION DURING SMALL SIDED GAMES

WORKLOAD EVALUATION DURING SMALL SIDED GAMES

Every individual involved with the physical development of players (e.g. technical, medical and conditioning staff) have their own views on the planning, design and execution of training programmes but whatever method is planned and used, the final target is to manage and manipulate the players fatigue and level of performance whilst minimising injury risk and ensuring freshness is restored pre-match. According to recent research by Owen et al, (2013) the physical and technical variables of certain game formats (3 v 3 to 11 v 11) in elite professional football needs to be understood and taken into consideration during the training design stage. Performing the correct type of games at specific times of the training week may enable technical, sports science and conditioning staff to maximally prepare players physically, technically and tactically, increasing the efficiency of training sessions.

Recently, both research and applied work surrounding *SSGs* has resulted in an increased knowledge regarding certain metabolic and physical demands characterising (Dellal et al, 2011; Owen et al, 2011; Hill-Haas et al, 2011), however, to date, the effects of football specific training games on players immune function and recovery is minimal (Thorpe and Sunderland, 2011; Sari-Sarraf et al, 2007). Within the realms of modern day football, failure to recover fully following training have been associated with the manifestation of *immunodepression* (a deficiency in one or more components of the immune system) in athletes (Neiman, 1994). Based on this suggestion within the elite level of the game, the training response and recovery monitoring is receiving greater attention than previously. Much of the available immunological research in elite athletes has focused primarily on post exercise salivary immune responses (Pedersen et al, 2000); with athletes experiencing a transitory decrease in immune function from 3 up to 72 hours post strenuous training or competition (Pedersen and Ullum, 1995). It is during this 'open window' period of immune depression, as proposed

by Nieman's' J shaped' relationship (Neiman, 1994), that athletes are considered to be at greatest risk of developing an upper respiratory tract infection (*URTI*) - throat and chest infections. As indicated previously, *SSGs* are a strenuous training intervention and manipulation of key variables leads to increased physical exertions which may leave the players in a state of immune depression. Based on this notion the players workload and intensity must be planned, monitored and evaluated in order to ensure the correct stimulus is being applied at the correct time.

While there is clear evidence of an association between *immunosuppression* (the partial or complete suppression of the immune response of an individual), volume and duration of exercise respectively within the literature, (Nakamura et al, 2006), the influence of intensity of exercise and its interaction with volume and duration of training need further clarification. Hard demanding training such as *SSGs* may compromise *mucosal immunity* (the study of the immune system that provides protection to an organism's mucous membrane). Engaging in bouts of high intensity and or high volume training for a prolonged time may cause decreases in *s-IgA concentrations* (salivary immunoglobulin-A which is part of the adaptive immune response), thus leaving athletes susceptible to picking up infections or muscle injuries. One day in between matches and or consecutive intense training may be inadequate for full recovery and thus leave players susceptible to illness or injury. As a result, the planning of training sessions inclusive of specific sided training games (i.e. volume x intensity) needs to be done with care to ensure the right stimulus is provided at the right time. Ensuring the correct pitch sizes, player numbers and bout durations are applied is the key to maintaining correct player preparation.

Football Conditioning: A Modern Scientific Approach

The continued development of *GPS* and *HR* monitors have now enabled coaches to assess 'live' or 'real time' training measurements during training sessions. The data (*TDC*, *HIDC*, sprint distance) obtained within *SSGs* through a live feed can then assist in managing the correct intensity and subsequent loading values imposed upon the players to limit the injury potential through excessive fatigue levels. This also allows technical and conditioning staff the opportunity to add specific changes during the session with the aim of gaining the required intensity.

5. LIMITATIONS OF SMALL SIDED GAMES

LIMITATIONS OF SMALL SIDED GAMES

Undeniably, several studies have shown how the physiological responses of *SSG* formats can be modified by manipulating key variables such as technical and tactical parameters (Abrantes et al, 2012) such as pitch size (Casamichana and Castellano, 2010; Owen et al, 2004), player numbers (Hill-Haas et al., 2010), bout duration (Franchini et al, 2010), scoring methods (Duarte, et al., 2010) and coach encouragement (Rampinini et al, 2007). Nevertheless, based on its emergence as a useful training method for aerobic-fitness and technical/tactical skill development (Dellal et al, 2008; Owen et al, 2011), when compared to actual match play, there are suggestions that *SSGs* may be unable to replicate the high-intensity and repeated sprint demands (Gabbett and Mulvey, 2008; Casamichana et al, 2012). These findings are reinforced by potential ceiling effects associated with a failure to achieve high intensities in players retaining either high aerobic endurance capacities or technical competency (Buchheit et al, 2009). Despite the extensive research into the physical, technical and movement profiles of *SSGs* (4 v 4) and their use within football (Little and Williams, 2007), our understanding of how to maximise their function at the elite level is not complete. Previous research has discussed the physiological responses of *SSG* in isolation, however, the implementation of these games should be carefully considered as part of an advanced planning structure (Owen et al, 2012) which may be more representative of the day-to-day activities within a professional football club.

As identified within the literature, high intensity running and sprint demands are more associated with match-play or *LSG* (11 v 11) formats (Hill-Haas et al, 2009). This may be a result of *LSGs* being played on significantly increased pitch sizes in conjunction with the fact that players in these game formats have less involvement with the ball (Owen et al, 2011). Alongside these pitch sizes and less ball involvement, the *LSG* formats generally result in an increased amount of high intensity running or sprinting when

out of possession or 'off the ball' movements in order to lose opponents or create scoring opportunities.

The limitations of *SSGs* as a sole training practice within the elite level of professional football is a recent research investigation conducted by Owen et al (2013). Within this study, the authors compared the technical activity and physical movements of various sided games within professional football. Furthermore, the study also examined the test-retest reliability of a range of sided-games varying from small, medium and large sided games. It was shown that *SSGs* have a significantly faster playing speed (metres per minute) when compared to *MSGs* and *LSGs* but significantly less high-intensity efforts, high-intensity running, and sprint distance when compared to *LSGs*. These reduced values of high speed and sprint distances within *SSGs* are suggested to be associated with the reduced opportunities to sprint into areas, due to the smaller pitch and the greater levels of technical competency needed. Findings also revealed significant differences between *SSGs*, *MSGs* and *LSGs* in technical demands (passes, dribbles, shots, headers). Dellal et al, (2012) has also described several limitations regarding the use of *SSGs* during training which should be taken into consideration. Small sided games may potentially affect team performance due to playing within smaller pitch areas, which leads to short and medium distance passes, which may be less useful for teams with a direct style (long passes) of play.

In addition, another limitation has been reported by previous studies when stating that *SSGs* show a greater individual coefficient of variation (Dellal et al, 2008) when assessing *HR* within *SSGs*. It was revealed from this study that *HR* responses from football players were less constant during *SSGs* when compared to intermittent running. The reason for these variations is due to the total uncontrolled nature of the games. Specific movements made by players within the games differ depending on players experience, positional roles during competitive matches, opposition players

Football Conditioning: A Modern Scientific Approach

movements, and/or their motivation (Spalding et al, 2004; Stolen, 2005).

The topic of injury risk within **SSGs** is very limited in terms of scientific literature. In this context, it is unknown if **SSGs** are associated with higher or lower risk of injury compared to other types of football specific training. Based on the higher contacts between players within this training setting, it would be expected that **SSGs** are associated with higher contact injuries compared to classical running intermittent training. As there is no scientific literature supporting this notion to date, the author strongly advises that **SSGs** be performed within the correct area sizes and rules in possession to limit the risk of injury.

Figure 31. Physical vs. Small Sided Game Continuum.

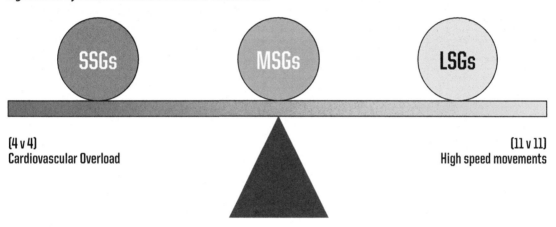

SSGs = Small Sided Games (4 v 4)

MSGs = Medium Sided Games (5 v 5 to 8 v 8)

LSGs = Large Sided Games (9 v 9 to 11 v 11)

CHAPTER SUMMARY

CHAPTER SUMMARY

PHYSICAL AND PHYSIOLOGICAL DEMANDS OF SSGs

- *SSGs* are seen as a multi-functional, time efficient training strategy that allows for the development of many key football components in conjunction with each other rather than in isolation (e.g. technical, tactical and physical).

- Generally, irrespective of positional roles, games are played at an average speed of 111 m/min to 133 m/min. In light of this, when the focus is to train at 'game intensity', coaches should ensure training games induce a speed of play equal to or greater than 111 m/min.

- There are significantly higher heart rate (*HR*) values in *SSGs* when compared to match play for all playing positions.

- Overall, the recent studies discussing the use of *SSGs* as a way of positively influencing players' football performance capabilities demonstrate that implementing a periodized *SSG* training intervention not only creates the same physical benefits of generic, non-football specific sessions but has the potential to significantly enhance physical profiles at the elite level.

- Being able to develop physical characteristics in conjunction to the technical and tactical elements of the game makes *SSGs* an appealing training methodology for fitness coaches, players, and technical coaches alike.

- *SSG* training may overload, and continually stress the body in order to increase the efficiency and subsequently improve a player's ability to recover from maximal exertions during the course of the game, shown through the improvement in RSA.

- *SSGs* have a significantly faster playing speed when compared to *MSGs* and *LSGs* but significantly less high-intensity efforts, high-speed running, and sprint distance when compared to *LSGs*.

- *SSGs* have been reported to increase players' motivation when compared to generic running intervals, eliciting the same overall *HR* response.

VARIABLES AFFECTING SSGs INTENSITY

- Manipulation of key variables within *SSGs* have a direct consequence on the physiological, technical and tactical components (i.e. number of players, pitch dimensions, game rules, bout duration and coach encouragement).

- The pitch dimensions play a fundamental role in the physical and technical demand imposed on players (i.e. the greater the pitch size per player numbers, the increased physical demand).

- Organisation of training sessions should ensure that pitch sizes be carefully considered in order to achieve the training objective and physical outcomes.

- In larger areas, the physical activity and requirements are increased, but the technical difficulty decreases.

- *SSGs* played with a limitation of 1/2 touches increased high-intensity running and the difficulty to perform technical actions (more specific to match demands).

Football Conditioning: A Modern Scientific Approach

- Coaches need to understand the different physiological demands imposed upon players within *SSGs*, especially if they include rule changes in relation to possession within the session. Additionally, coaches should also have an understanding regarding the physical, physiological and technical differences between positional roles.

- If the main target of the session is to develop physical and technical components in isolation or in conjunction to each other, then the correct pitch sizes must be utilised.

- Games with a small numbers of players can deliver a more effective technical training stimulus, due to the overload in technical actions being increased in accordance to the reduction in player numbers

- Specific *SSGs* may be better suited for the technical demands of midfield or forward players as they create more opportunities to dribble, tackle and shoot in accordance to the increased touches and/or involvement with the ball.

- It may be more appropriate for defenders to develop technically and tactically with *LSGs* based on the research suggesting these game types give players more opportunity to block, intercept and perform aerial challenges.

- The intensity of a *SSG* can be significantly increased when using man-marking tactics.

PERIODIZATION OF SMALL SIDED GAMES

- Periodization and its capacity to plan and design a schedule with the appropriate training load (intensity, volume, and frequency) play a key factor when attempting to avoid injury and enhance physical and technical performance.

- Advanced planning between technical, conditioning and medical staff is vital in order to elicit the correct volume, duration, and intensity of training and ensure maximum player freshness pre-game

- It should be highlighted that being able to develop physical characteristics in conjunction to the technical and tactical elements of the game, within a relatively short period of time, makes *SSGs* an appealing proposition for players and coaches alike in their aim of developing physical profiles and subsequent performance.

WORKLOAD

- Performing the correct type of games at specific times of the training week may enable technical, sports science and conditioning staff to maximally prepare players physically, technically and tactically, increasing the efficiency of training sessions.

- The continued development of *GPS* and *HR* monitors have now enabled coaches to assess 'live' or 'real time' training measurements during training sessions. The data (total distance covered, high intensity distance covered, sprint distance) obtained within *SSGs* through a live feed can then assist in managing the correct intensity and subsequent loading values imposed upon the players to limit the injury potential through excessive fatigue levels. This also allows technical and conditioning staff the opportunity to add specific changes during the session with the aim of gaining the required intensity

Football Conditioning: A Modern Scientific Approach

CHAPTER 3

SMALL SIDED GAMES (TRAINING DRILLS)

PRACTICE FORMAT

Each practice includes clear diagrams with supporting training notes such as:

- Name of Practice
- Objective of Practice
- Description of Practice
- Variation or Progression (if applicable)
- Coaching Points

KEY

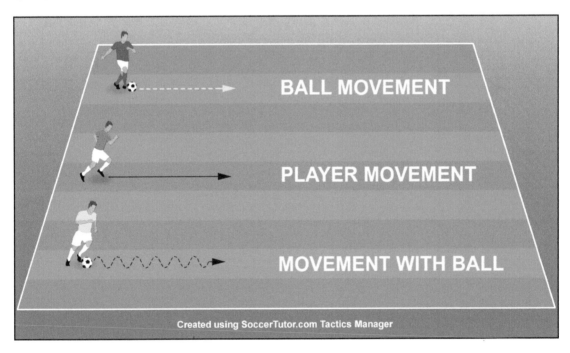

BALL MOVEMENT

PLAYER MOVEMENT

MOVEMENT WITH BALL

Created using SoccerTutor.com Tactics Manager

Football Conditioning: A Modern Scientific Approach

Playing Through the Lines in a Possession Game with Goalkeepers

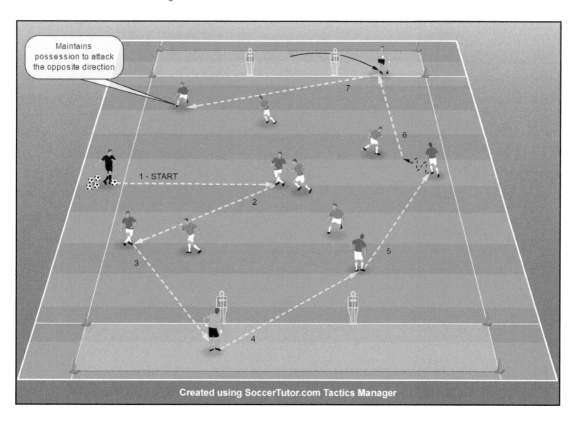

Maintains possession to attack the opposite direction

1 - START

Created using SoccerTutor.com Tactics Manager

Description

In this practice we play 5 v 5 in the central area (30 x 35 yards) and we also have 2 x 8 yard zones with neutral goalkeepers positioned behind 2 mannequins as shown in the diagram. The aim for both teams is to maintain possession and to continually play from one end to the other. Each time they pass from one goalkeeper to the other without the opposition intercepting the ball they score 1 point. Play in 3 minute periods.

Variations: 1) Challenge the players to complete a set number of passes to score a point. 2) You can use multiple player numbers to change the demand on players, but the key theme is on the tactical demand.

Progression: Players are not allowed to close goalkeepers in possession - progress to allow pressure.

Coaching Points

1. Players need to demonstrate quality of movement in order to play into and receive from the goalkeeper.

2. Ensure a high intensity of play is maintained within the game through pressure.

3. The players should look to switch play and play through the pitch.

4. Ensure the defending team do not stay in deep areas to try and block the goalkeeper.

3 Team 4 v 4 (+4) Directional Play Possession Game

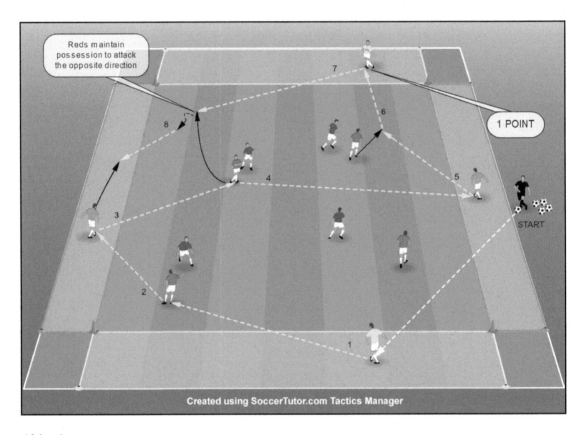

Reds maintain possession to attack the opposite direction

1 POINT

START

Created using SoccerTutor.com Tactics Manager

Objective

We work on directional based possession with the aim of maximising the workload (conditioning).

Description

The players are organised into 3 teams of 4 players with a 4 v 4 in the 30 x 30 yard area and 4 players on the outside. The players inside the area are limited to 3 touches and the outside players are limited to 1 touch. Play in 3 minute periods.

The players look to maintain possession and a point is scored when the ball is played from one end to the other and both of the central outside players (yellows) have touched the ball. Maintaining possession but focussing the passage of play towards an end player leads to high intensity directional play with a strong purpose.

Coaching Points

1. The players need to demonstrate good quality of movement in order to maintain possession, the correct body position to receive and play - focus direction of play towards the outside players (yellows and oranges).

2. Encourage the use of one-two combinations with the outside players to increase the speed of play.

Football Conditioning: A Modern Scientific Approach

Playing Through the Midfield in a 5 v 5 (3 v 3) Directional Possession Game

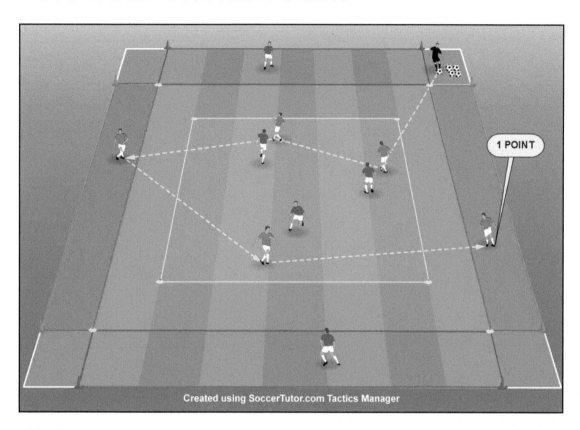

1 POINT

Created using SoccerTutor.com Tactics Manager

Objective

This is a directional based possession game with a focus on midfield rotation. The aim is to maximise the workload of the players (conditioning).

Description

In a total area of 35 x 35 yards we mark out a 25 x 25 yard square inside. We play a 5 v 5 game with 3 v 3 (midfield 3) inside the smaller square and 2 players outside (1 at each opposite end who are limited to 2 touches). Play 5 x 3 minute periods.

The players maintain possession and score a point by passing the ball from one outside player to the other.

Coaching Points

1. Maintaining possession and switching play through the midfield players is key and so is the rotation of the midfield 3 in order to open up space to play the ball forwards.

2. The players need to demonstrate good movement and the correct body position to receive and play.

3. Limit the outside players to 1 touch to increase the speed of play.

4. This practice can be used with more or less players depending on the focus of the session.

Football Conditioning: A Modern Scientific Approach

Possession Play and Third Man Runs in a 7 v 7 Small Sided Game with End Zones

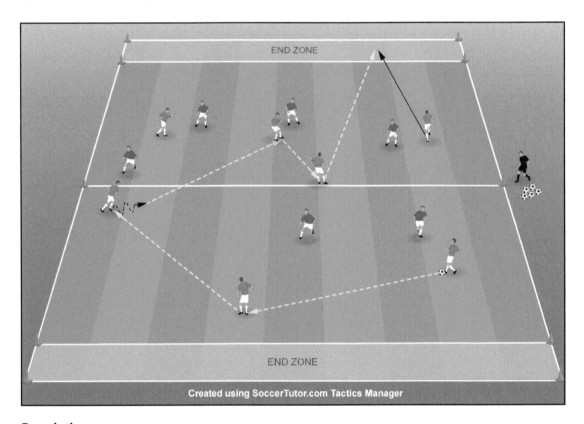

END ZONE

END ZONE

Created using SoccerTutor.com Tactics Manager

Description

In a 50 x 60 yard area, we play 7 v 7. We have two end zones that are 8 yards in depth. The aim for both teams is to maintain possession, play through lines and score a goal by one player receiving the ball within the end zone. The team in possession must create space for third man runners to exploit. Players on the defending team are not allowed in the end zone.

Progressions

1. A goal is only allowed if all the players on the attacking team are in the attacking half.

2. Make a team complete a set amount of passes before being allowed to score - draw opposition to press the ball which will create space in behind.

Coaching Points

1. This requires patience in possession to draw opposition players in before playing penetrating passes.

2. This practice can be used with more or less players depending on the focus of the session.

3. Timing of games and area size can be changed to suit but different physical outputs will be achieved.

4. Players in possession need to attack the end zone - strongly encourage the use of third man runs.

Football Conditioning: A Modern Scientific Approach

Utilising the Goalkeeper in a Dynamic Possession Game

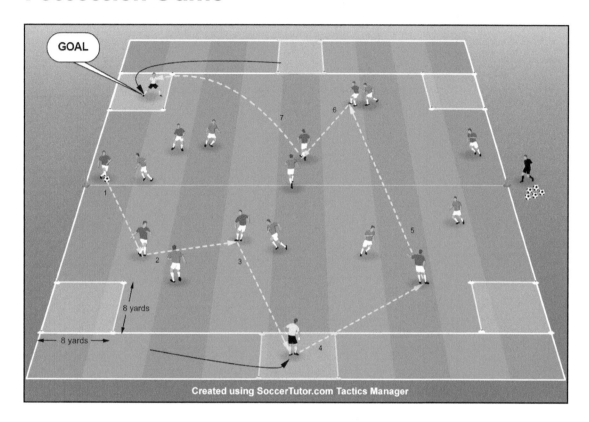

GOAL

8 yards

8 yards

Created using SoccerTutor.com Tactics Manager

Objective

We work on directional possession with the involvement of the goalkeepers. The aim is to maximise the workload of the players (conditioning).

Description

In a 55 x 55 yard area, we mark out 6 zones (8 x 8 yards) as shown in the diagram. We play a 9 v 9 game with two neutral goalkeepers who are free to move into any of the 3 zones at their end. Play 5 minute periods.

The first aim is to maintain possession and all players are limited to 3 touches. If the ball is passed into the middle zone (yellow), it must be to the goalkeeper's feet. If the ball is passed into one of the side zones (white), it must be played into the goalkeeper's hands. This creates an additional thought process for this possession game.

A goal is scored by passing to one goalkeeper at one end and then playing to the opposite end to the other goalkeeper successfully (without the ball being intercepted.

Progressions

1. A goal is only allowed if all players on the attacking team are in the attacking half when the keeper receives.

2. Make a team complete a set amount of passes before being allowed to score - draw opposition to press them.

123

Football Conditioning: A Modern Scientific Approach

Coaching Points

1. Ensure a high ball speed, quality of movement to maintain possession, timing and quality of passing/runs.

2. Look for quick switches of play, only using 1-2 touches in possession.

3. Good decision making is required to determine the correct type of pass.

4. The goalkeeper must stay active and move between zones to ensure players have an easy passing option and goal scoring opportunities.

5. This practice can be used with more or less players depending on the focus of the session.

6. Timing of games and area size can be changed to suit but different physical outputs will be achieved.

Continuous High Intensity 3 v 3 Duels

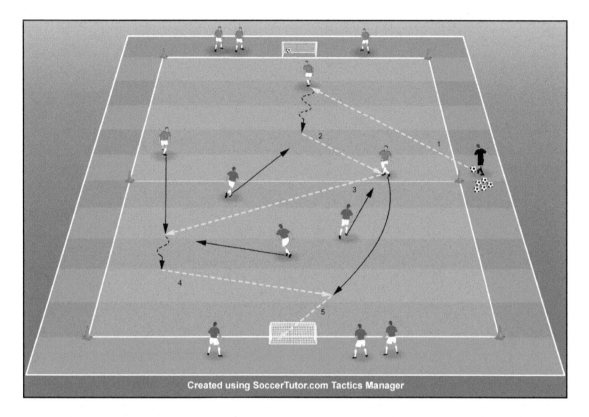

Description

The players are organised into 4 teams of 3 players (2 teams in red / 2 teams in blue). 2 teams compete (3 v 3) within the area with the aim of maintaining possession and creating opportunities to score in the mini goal. The other 2 teams are positioned behind the goals (recovery time).

The first two teams play for 1 minute. After the minute is up the next 2 teams enter the pitch and play against each other. The 2 teams that were playing walk behind the goal to recover for 1 minute.

Progressions

1. A goal is only allowed if all players on the attacking team are in the attacking half when they score.

2. Make a team complete a set amount of passes before being allowed to score - draw opposition to press the ball which will create space in behind.

Coaching Points

1. Ensure there is a high intensity and fast ball speed, good quality of movement and intense pressure on the ball carriers at all times.

2. Players should focus on quick passes, overlaps and checking away to create space to dribble and finish.

125

High Intensity Pressing and Quick Shooting in a 4 v 4 Attack vs Defence Practice

Objective

We play a 4 v 4 small sided game with continued pressure to increase the heart rate (*HR*) and physical work output; the players must press at a high intensity.

Description

The players are organised into 3 teams of 4 players (reds, blues and yellows) and we also have a goalkeeper defending his goal. The teams are split into 3 roles - attackers (red), defenders (blue) and feeders (yellow) outside the area.

Each feeder player (yellow) has 5 balls in the positions shown and they are given a number (1-4). The coach calls out a number and that player passes the ball to an attacking player who tries to shoot quickly. The attacking team keep working to score goals until all the balls are used up (7 minutes maximum). Once the attacking team has finished, they become feeders, the feeders become defenders and the defenders become attackers.

Variations

1. Introduce a time limit to score to increase the intensity and limit the number of touches used.

2. Create an 8 v 4 situation with the outside players providing support.

Coaching Points

1. Attacking players must look to check away and create space to receive.

2. If an attacker is unable to shoot quickly he should look for quick passes and overlapping runs should be made.

Fast Speed of Play in a 7 v 7 Four Goal Small Sided Game

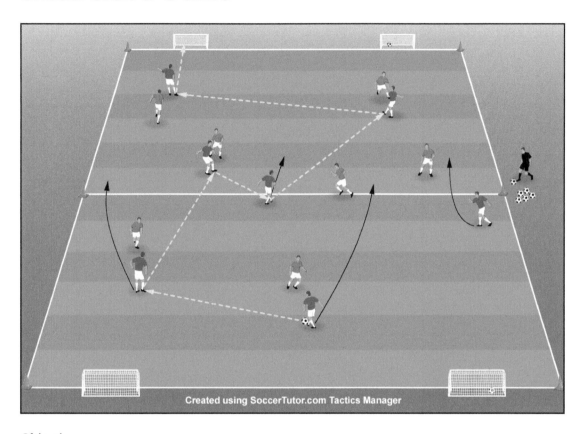

Created using SoccerTutor.com Tactics Manager

Objective

The emphasis is on quick play and high ball speed in this 7 v 7 small sided game to improve the aerobic capacity, speed endurance and to maximise the workload (conditioning).

Description

In a 50 x 60 yard are, we play a 7 v 7 small sided game with 4 mini goals (each team attacks 2 goals). The two teams aim to maintain possession and create opportunities to score. Play 6 minute periods.

The players are limited to 3 touches throughout but must score with 1 touch.

Progressions

1. A goal is only allowed if all players on the attacking team are in the attacking half when they score.

2. Make a team complete a set amount of passes before being allowed to score - draw opposition to press the ball which will create space in behind.

Football Conditioning: A Modern Scientific Approach

Fast Speed of Play and Pressing in an 8 v 8 Possession Game with Goalkeepers

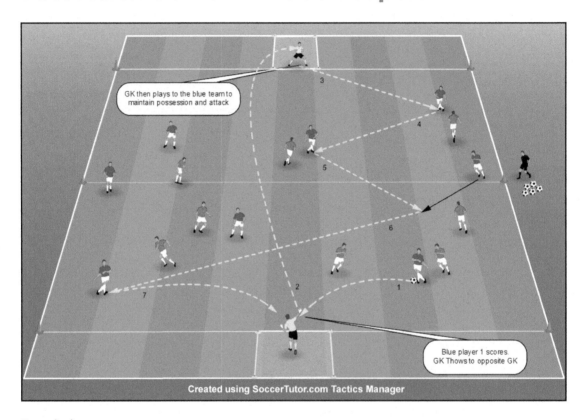

GK then plays to the blue team to maintain possession and attack

Blue player 1 scores.
GK Thows to opposite GK

Created using SoccerTutor.com Tactics Manager

Description

In a 40 x 45 yard area, we play a 10 minute 8 v 8 game with 2 zones outside with goalkeepers positioned in them. The outfield players aim to maintain possession and create opportunities to play in the attacking half of the pitch. Goals are scored by playing into the goalkeeper's hands within the zone. The goalkeeper then throws the ball to the opposite keeper who passes to the scoring team to start a new attack.

Progressions

1. A goal is only allowed if all players on the attacking team are in the attacking half when they score.

2. Make a team complete a set amount of passes (10) before being allowed to score - draw opposition to press the ball to open up areas to play through.

Coaching Points

1. Ensure there is a high intensity and fast ball speed, good quality of movement and intense pressure on the ball carriers at all times.

2. Players should focus on quick passes, overlaps and checking away to create space to pass to the goalkeeper.

3. The defending team need to maintain a positional shape, pressure the ball carrier and block passing lanes.

Football Conditioning: A Modern Scientific Approach

6 (+2) v 6 (+2) Possession Game with Quick Changes of Position

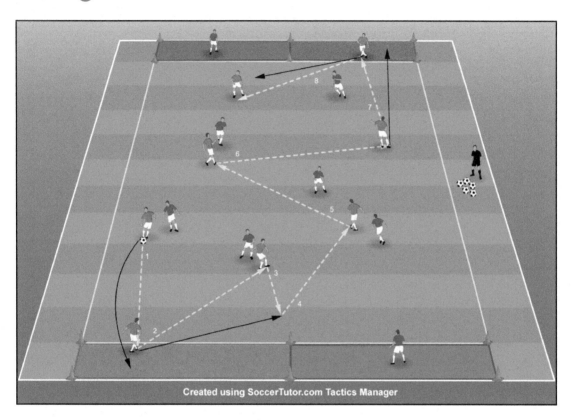

Created using SoccerTutor.com Tactics Manager

Objective

We work on high speed of play and intense pressing within a possession game.

Description

In a 45 x 55 yard area, we play 6 v 6 inside and have 2 extra players for each team outside in the positions shown. Players within the area aim to maintain possession and play the ball from one outside player to the other without the opposition intercepting the ball (1 goal).

When the end player receives he moves into the area and the player who made the pass moves to the outside. The players are limited to 3 touches throughout. Play 3 minute periods.

Progression: Make a team complete a set amount of passes (10) before being allowed to score - draw opposition to press the ball to open up areas to play through.

Coaching Points

1. Players should focus on quick passes, forward runs, overlaps and creating space to pass to the outside players.

2. The defending team need to press the ball, prevent passes to outside players, stop series of passes and maintain a positional shape to make the practice more game realistic.

Football Conditioning: A Modern Scientific Approach

7 v 7 Dynamic Small Sided Game with Mini Goals and Cone Gates

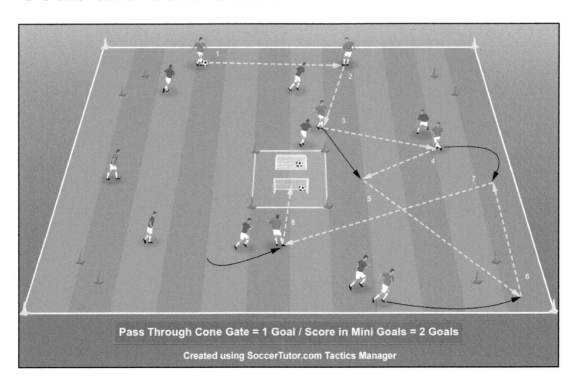

Pass Through Cone Gate = 1 Goal / Score in Mini Goals = 2 Goals

Created using SoccerTutor.com Tactics Manager

Objective

A directional based possession game with the focus on creating space and exploiting it. The aim is to maximise the workload (conditioning).

Description

In a 40 x 60 yard area, we have 2 goals in the centre, 4 cone gates in the corners and play a 7 v 7 game.

The teams aim to keep possession and then score by either playing a successful pass through one of the cone gates (1 goal) or scoring in one of the mini goals (2 goals).

Progression: Make a team complete a set amount of passes before being allowed to score - draw opposition to press the ball to open up areas to play through.

Coaching Points

1. Ensure there is a high intensity and fast ball speed, good quality of movement and intense pressure on the ball carriers at all times.

2. Encourage the use of quick switches of play to open up the opposition.

3. Quick support play is needed when the ball is switched to the other side.

4. The defending team need to press the ball, prevent passes to outside players, stop series of passes and maintain a positional shape to make the practice more game realistic.

5. The defending team must defend the central area of the pitch, whilst also being able to cover the cone gates.

Football Conditioning: A Modern Scientific Approach

CHAPTER 4

TRANSITION GAMES

3 Team Dynamic Zonal Transition Game

To score, all blues must be in the attacking half

Transition quickly - attack the reds and score in the opposite half

Created using SoccerTutor.com Tactics Manager

Objective

To improve the players' capability in the transition from defence to attack (speed endurance /aerobic capacity).

Description

We have 3 teams of 5 players (+ 2 goalkeepers) in a 35 x 50 yard area. We start with one team (yellow) attacking a second team (blue) within one half. The attacking team attempt to score – if successful they receive the ball back and turn to attack the other goal (vs. reds). If the yellows lose possession to the blues at any time (as shown in the diagram example), they stay in that half and the blues immediately attack the reds in the opposite half.

We have constant and continuous transitional waves of attack. You can use multiple players or extra teams to change the demand on players and allow for rest. Play 5 minute periods.

Coaching Points

1. The focus is on the reaction of the players to transition from defensive duties to attacking (tactical demand).

2. Commit defenders and attack at speed. Change the pace and increase speed of play on turnover of possession.

End to End Possession and Intense Pressing (3 v 7) in a Transition Game

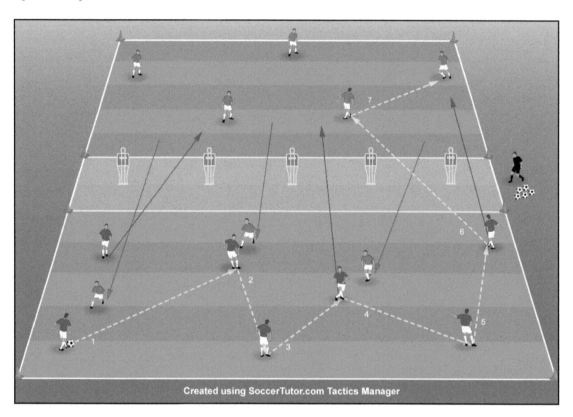

Created using SoccerTutor.com Tactics Manager

Description

In a 40 x 60 yard area we have 2 end zones (40 x 25 yards) and one central zone (40 x 10 yards) with 5 mannequins positioned as shown. We start with one team (blues - all 7 players) in an end zone. On the coach's whistle 3 red players move to pressure the blues and create a 7 v 3 situation. The blues aim to keep possession for a set number of passes before passing the ball past the mannequins to the opposite side (1 point). The reds then start in possession and 3 blue players move across to create the same 7 v 3 situation. Play 5 minute periods.

If the reds win possession or the ball goes out of play they score 1 point and If they win possession and play a pass through two of the mannequins to their teammates they score 2 points. The 3 red players then move to the opposite zone to join their teammates in possession. The team with the most points at the end wins.

Variations: 1) The game can be made easier or more difficult by changing the number of defending players.
2) You can also change the number of touches allowed to increase the intensity and difficulty.

Coaching Points

1. Ensure quality of movement and technique in order to maintain possession, speed and intensity of pressing and quick reactions for the transition from defence to attack (or attack to defence).

2. Ensure there is high ball speed in possession and the players press and chase as a unit.

Football Conditioning: A Modern Scientific Approach

8 v 8 Transition Game - Keep Possession in Larger Area / Press in a Smaller Area

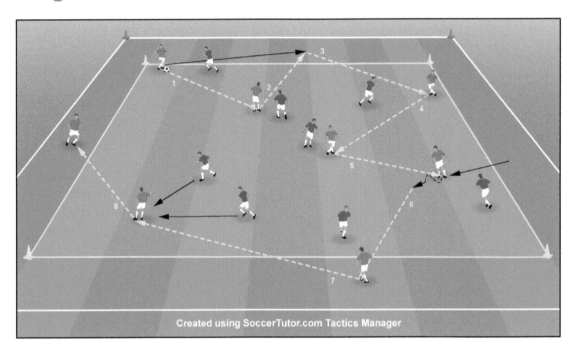

Created using SoccerTutor.com Tactics Manager

Objective

We play a possession based game with the aim of improving the players' capability in the transition phase. The aim is to maximise the workload (conditioning).

Description

In a total area of 60 x 60 yards, we have a zone inside which is 55 x 55 yards. We play a 9 v 9 possession game. The team in possession can open up the pitch and maintain possession in the full area but the defending team can only play within the smaller area. If possession is lost, the teams switch roles. Play 4 minute periods.

All passes from outside of the smaller square must be played into the smaller square. Defending players are not allowed to enter the larger square - they remain compact and mark the potential receivers tightly to try and win the ball when it is played through the smaller square.

Progression: You can limit the number of touches within the larger square or allow 1 defending player in there to add pressure.

Coaching Points

1. Ensure quality of movement and technique and high intensity of pressing is applied within the smaller square.
2. The team in possession need to make the pitch as big as possible to utilise their advantage.
3. Focus on the quick reactions needed of the players in the transition from defence to attack (or vice versa).
4. The teams need to stay compact and hunt the ball together if they lose possession.

Football Conditioning: A Modern Scientific Approach

Pressing to Win the Ball Back Quickly in an 8 v 4 Transition Game

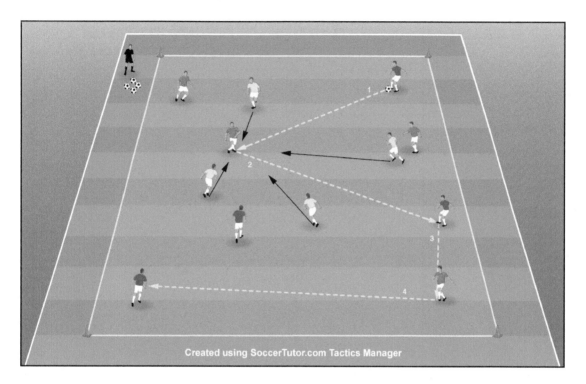

Created using SoccerTutor.com Tactics Manager

Objective

The aim of this practice is to react quickly to losing the ball and press in groups to win the ball back quickly. This should be done at a high tempo to work on speed endurance and develop the aerobic capacity.

Description

In a 35 x 35 yard area, we have 3 teams of 4 players. 2 teams play together and aim to maintain possession (reds and blues in the diagram) and the other team try to win the ball (yellows) which creates an 8 v 4 situation. The team that loses possession then becomes the defending team and they must ensure they make a quick transition, working in a group to try and win the ball back as quickly as possible. Play 3 minute periods.

The aim of the game is to ensure a continued transition of possession. You can start by having the teams defend for a set period of time so the players become familiar with the game before introducing the continuous cycle. The players are limited to 2 touches throughout (reduce to 1 touch to increase the intensity of play).

Coaching Points

1. Ensure quality of movement and technique in order to maintain possession, speed and intensity of pressing for the transition from defence to attack (or attack to defence).

2. The 2 teams in possession need to make the pitch as big as possible.

3. The players need quick reactions for the transition from attack to defence, making sure to stay compact and hunt the ball together.

Pressing to Win the Ball Back Quickly in a 6 v 6 (+6) Transition Game

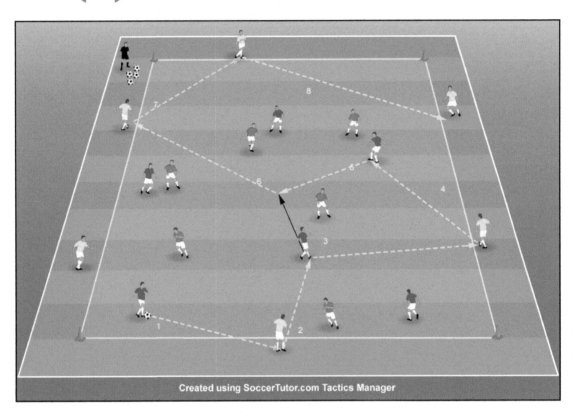

Created using SoccerTutor.com Tactics Manager

Objective

A possession based game with the aim of developing the transitions (conditioning / aerobic capacity).

Description

In a 40 x 40 yard area, we have 3 teams of 6 players. One team is positioned on the outside (yellows) and they try to keep possession with another team on the inside (blues). The third team (reds) try to win the ball which creates a 12 v 6 situation.

The team that loses the ball becomes the defending team so there is a constant transition from opening the pitch up to maintain possession vs. staying compact and making the pitch small in order to regain possession.

You can start by having the teams defend for a set period of time so the players become familiar with the game before introducing the continuous cycle. The inside players are limited to 3 touches (reduce to 2 touches to increase the intensity of play) and the outside players are limited to 1 touch throughout.

Coaching Points

1. The team in possession use the outside players to keep possession and make the pitch as big as possible.
2. The defending team stay compact and press as a unit to try and win the ball.

136

Intense Pressing (2 v 4) in a 3 Team Transition Game

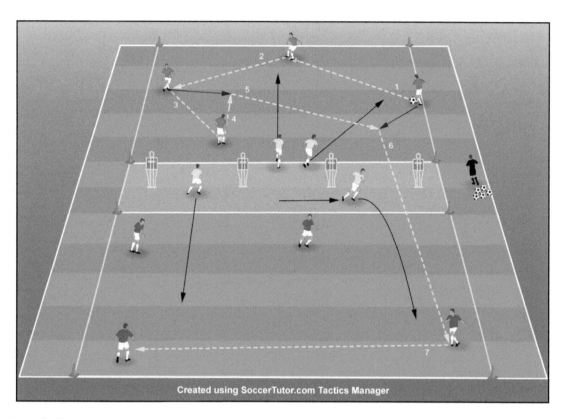

Created using SoccerTutor.com Tactics Manager

Description

In a 20 x 35 yard area we have 2 end zones (20 x 15 yards each) and 1 middle zone (20 x 5 yards) with 4 mannequins in the positions shown. We have 3 teams of 4 players and each team starts in one of the zones.

The practice starts with one team keeping possession in an end zone (reds in diagram) and 2 defending players (yellows) move from the middle zone to press and try to win the ball or kick the ball out of play (1 point). If the 2 yellow players are successful then the red and yellow teams switch roles. Play 5 minute periods.

If the reds manage to complete a set number of passes they must then attempt to play a pass to the other side past the mannequins and the 2 yellow middle zone players (who can attempt to stop the ball) or chip a pass over them. If they successfully pass to the team on the other side (blues) they score 1 point and the 2 yellow middle zone players move across to press and try to win the ball (the other 2 yellow players move into the middle zone).

The players are limited to 2 touches throughout.

Coaching Points

1. There should be a constant change over of possession and defending players working into and out of the middle zone - this tests the players' speed endurance and stamina.

2. If the same team are defending for too long, change the roles to allow the players to recover.

Football Conditioning: A Modern Scientific Approach

Possession and Switching Play in a 2 Zone Transition Game

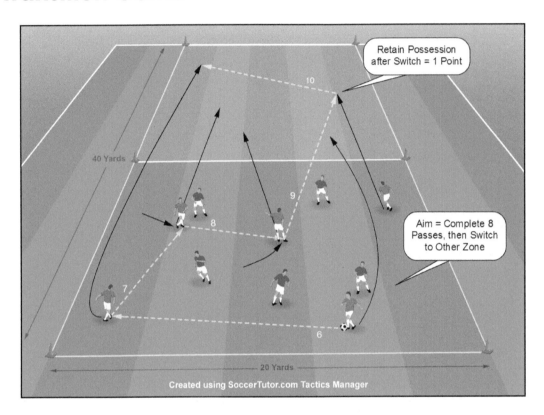

> Retain Possession after Switch = 1 Point

> Aim = Complete 8 Passes, then Switch to Other Zone

40 Yards

20 Yards

Created using SoccerTutor.com Tactics Manager

Description

In a 20 x 40 yard area, we shave 2 equal zones and play 5 v 5. Both teams start in one zone and the team in possession try to complete 8 consecutive passes and the other team tries to win the ball or kick it our of play. Play 2.5 minute periods.

If 8 passes are completed without any interceptions, one player (red player in diagram) must move across to the other zone to receive the next pass. All the players on the red team then also move across and if possession is retained, the team score 1 point (successful switch of play). If the defending team (blues) win the ball or the ball goes out of play, the blues start with the ball and aim to complete 8 passes before switching play themselves.

Variations: 1) Limit the touches or increase the set amount of passes to change the intensity of the practice.
2) Increase the number of players to decrease the intensity (or vice versa) - depending on the physical outcome.

Coaching Points

1. Ensure quality of movement and technique in order to maintain possession, speed and intensity of pressing for the transition from defence to attack (or attack to defence).

2. The team in possession need to focus on making the pitch as big as possible, utilising all the space.

3. The speed of the support players is key in order to maximise the potential to maintain possession.

4. Do not force the switch of play pass - if it's not on then keep possession and play the ball when appropriate.

Possession Play and Quick Break Attacks in a 7 v 7 Game

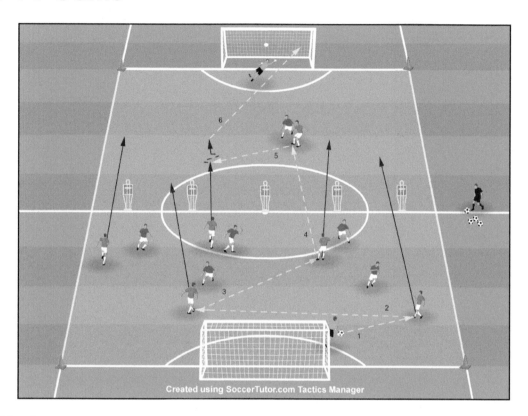

Created using SoccerTutor.com Tactics Manager

Objective

To regain possession and play beyond the press into the attacking phase (speed endurance / aerobic capacity).

Description

In a 60 x 45 yard area we position 5 mannequins on the halfway line and play 6 v 6 (+2 neutral GKs). The practice starts with a goalkeeper and a 5 v 5 situation in zone 1. There is 1 forward for each team in zone 2.

The team in possession (reds in diagram) must complete a set number of passes within zone 1 before playing to the forward in the other half - the intensity of the practice is influenced by the amount of passes required. All of the reds then move into zone 2 to make supporting runs and attack the goal. The blue defenders follow the attackers (track them) to defend the goal.

If the blues win the ball in zone 1 they immediately try and play to their forward, all make supporting runs and attack the goal. The red players follow the blues (track them) to defend the goal.

Coaching Points

1. The emphasis is initially on creating space and keeping good possession, then moves to quick support play.

2. Ensure a full press from the defending team to raise the intensity of the game.

3. Quick forward passing is needed in the transition. Switch play in final third, looking to move the opposition.

Dynamic 4 Zone 8 (+4) v 8 Possession Game

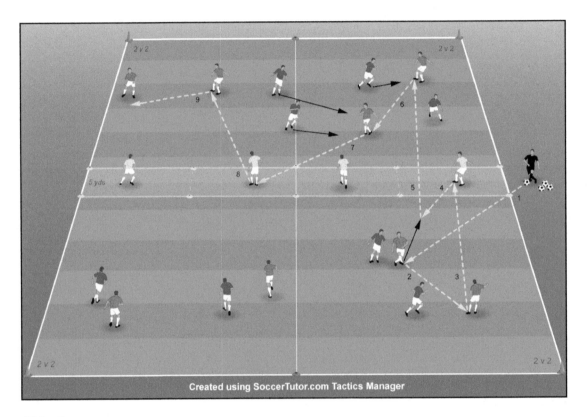

Created using SoccerTutor.com Tactics Manager

Objective

Winning and then securing/maintaining possession in a transition game (conditioning / aerobic capacity).

Description

In a 40 x 45 yard area we divide the pitch into 4 equal zones as shown. We play an 8 v 8 (+4) possession game. We start with 2 players from each team in each quarter and 4 neutral players who remain in the central area (5 yards) as shown, in order to retain a positional format to the game.

The team in possession must have 2 players per zone at all times in order to open up the pitch. The defending team can press collectively and try to win the ball. This transition game requires quick reactions as it constantly changes from pressing to opening up the pitch to keep possession.

Coaching Points

1. Maximise the overload with the spare players in possession (12 v 8 advantage).
2. Ensure collective pressing is used to try and regain possession.
3. Quick play is required when possession is won and through the transition.
4. The first reaction after regaining possession needs to be to open up the pitch and drop into the zones.

140

Football Conditioning: A Modern Scientific Approach

Quick Break Attacks in a 3 Team Small Sided Game

Yellows aim to win possession and then score quickly in either goal

Blues and Reds aim to keep possession (10 v 5)

Created using SoccerTutor.com Tactics Manager

Objective

We work on quick breaks after winning possession (maximising the workload and increasing the aerobic capacity.

Description

In a 40 x 50 yard area, we have 3 teams of 5 players + 2 neutral goalkeepers. 2 teams play together with the aim of maintaining possession. The defending team press together and try to win the ball.

If the defending team win the ball, they try to score as quickly as possible (in either goal) and the other players must react quickly and apply pressure to stop them scoring. The goalkeepers only become live when the ball has been won by the defending team.

The team that loses possession becomes the new defending team after the attack is finished.

Coaching Points

1. Quick reactions are needed for the transition from defence to attack and attack to defence.

2. In possession - retain the ball, with rotation of movement. Out of possession - press the ball.

3. Good and quick decision making is required in and out of possession.

141

3 v 3 (+2) Possession and Pressing Game

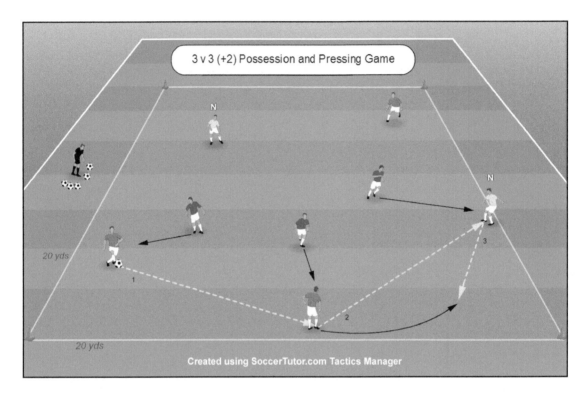

Objective: We work on winning possession with a numerical disadvantage. The aim is to develop the aerobic capacity of football players.

Description

In a 20 x 20 yard area, we play 3 v 3 (+2 neutral players) which creates a 5 v 3 advantage for the team in possession. The players play a possession game and the coach counts the number of passes each team can successfully complete in 2 minutes. The team with the greater total number of passes within the 2 minutes wins the game.

We play 4/5 x 2.5 minute games. The focus should be placed on the defending team shutting off angles of play and forcing the play in one direction so they are able to press and win the ball.

Variations

1. Increase the intensity, a team can score a point by completing a set number of passes.

2. Coaches can also change the number of players depending upon the focus of the session.

Coaching Points

1. Ensure quality of movement when in possession of the ball.

2. Ensure a high intensity of play is maintained within the game through pressure.

Playing Through the Centre in a Position Specific 4 Goal Game

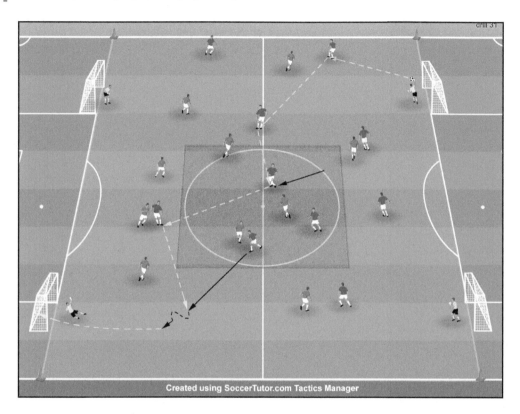

Created using SoccerTutor.com Tactics Manager

Objective: We play a position specific directional game with the aim of playing through the central zone. The aim is to maximise the workload (conditioning).

Description

We play a 10 v 10 game with 4 goals and 4 goalkeepers and mark out a central area as shown. Each team attacks and defends 2 goals. This can be adapted so that one team defends 1 central goal and attacks 2 wide goals - this all depends on the coach's focus. Ensure the players are played in their specific positional roles.

For a team to be able to score, they must first play through the central zone. This encourages quick switches of play with the focus on moving the opposition from side to side and creating/exploiting the space in wide areas.

Coaching Points

1. Use the goalkeepers to play out (numerical advantage in defending half of the pitch). Do not force the pass, be patient in the build-up.

2. Ensure a high intensity of play is maintained to replicate game-like pressure.

3. Look to play forward through the central zone. Players should rotate and drop in between the lines and the forwards should look to drop back into the central zone to help in the possession phase.

4. Switch play in attacking half – move the opposition. Wide forwards should commit players and break lines.

143

High Intensity Conditioning in Continuous 3 v 3 Possession Games

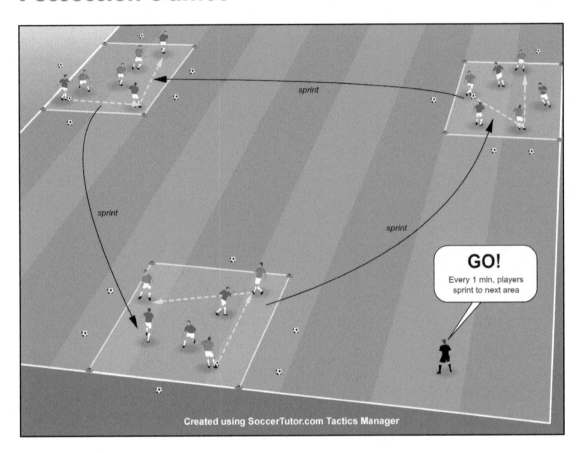

sprint

sprint

sprint

GO!
Every 1 min, players
sprint to next area

Created using SoccerTutor.com Tactics Manager

Objective

To develop the aerobic capacity of football players.

Description

We have 6 groups of 3 players. We play 3 v 3 in each of the 3 areas that we mark out (further areas can be added to involve more numbers). Ensure there are spare balls around the area for when the ball goes out.

We play this game in 5 minute intervals. Every minute, the coach shouts 'GO!' and all the players within an area sprint from one area to the next to continue the possession game. Once the 5 minutes is up, the players rest for a minimum of 2.5 minutes and a maximum of 5 minutes. There can be 3-6 repetitions, with the amount performed increasing as the players' fitness levels develop and increase over time.

A player's heart rate measured during training can be used to determine the exercise intensity at which the players are working. In this exercise, the players are performing high Intensity training – approx. 180 bpm which is 90% of their maximum heart rate (*HRM*). Training at this intensity will result in increased aerobic capabilities.

High Intensity Aerobic Endurance in a 5 v 5 Small Sided Game

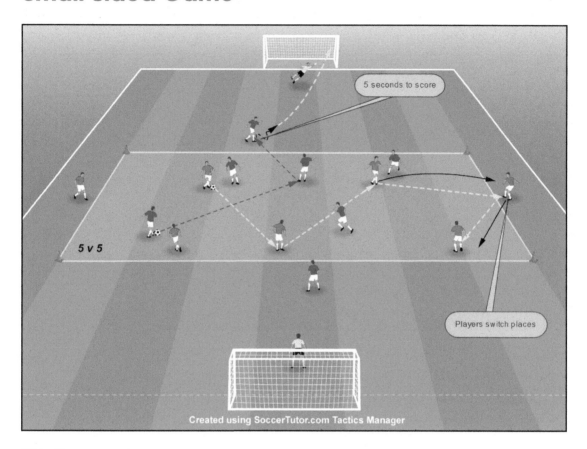

5 seconds to score

5 v 5

Players switch places

Created using SoccerTutor.com Tactics Manager

Objective

To develop the aerobic capacity of players within a football specific practice.

Description

We have a 5 v 5 situation in the central area and play with 2 balls. One team (blue) aims to score by playing into either of the 2 forwards outside the area who must score past the keeper within 5 seconds of receiving a pass.

The other team (red) aim to switch play from one side to the other. When the ball has been played to one of the 2 outside players, the player who played the pass switches places with him.

We play this game in 5 minute intervals. Once the 5 minutes is up, the players rest for a minimum of 2.5 minutes and a maximum of 5 minutes. Perform 3-6 repetitions. In this exercise, the players are performing high Intensity training – approx. 180 bpm which is 90% of their maximum heart rate (HRM). Training at this intensity will result in increased aerobic capabilities.

Coaching Point: The key technical elements are the interchanging of the players, good movement + the weight, timing and quality of passing.

Aerobic Endurance in a Dynamic 6 v 6 Transition Game

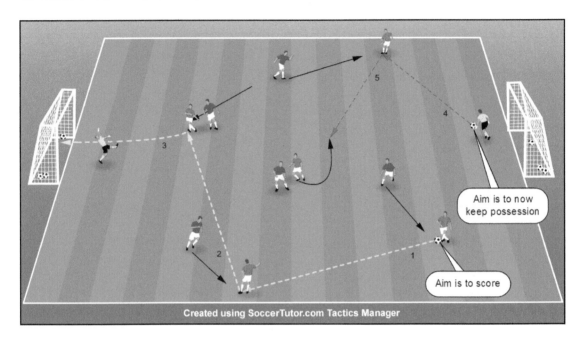

Created using SoccerTutor.com Tactics Manager

Objective

A possession based game with the main aim to work on transition play (conditioning / aerobic capacity).

Description

In a 40 x 30 yard area, we play a continuous 6 v 6 possession game (total duration of 30 minutes with rest time. The aim for the team in possession (reds) is to score a goal. If they score, their new aim becomes to keep possession for as long as possible. The opposing team (blues) press collectively and try to win the ball. If they win the ball they then have the same aims - first to score and then to maintain possession after scoring. This same sequence is continuous.

This particular practice involves the players working with a ball. This session was designed to include games that allow for the players heart rate to increase and be maintained at a level where it would allow for an improvement within the cardiovascular system (more than 85% of the maximum heart rate).

The total duration of this practice should be approximately 30 minutes, but there must be time for rest in between a multiple of games. This is seen as an intensive training game, therefore the duration of each game should not exceed 10 minutes. This then allows the players to work at 90% of their maximum heart rate.

Variations

1.   8 x 4 minute games.

2.   5 x 6 minute games.

3.   4 x 8 minute games.

4.   3 x 10 minute games.

Coaching Points

1. There needs to be high intensity and speed of pressure applied by the defending team.

2. Focus on the reaction of the players in the transition from defence to attack and vice versa.

3. Ensure quality of movement and make the pitch as big as possible in order to maintain possession.

4. There needs to be a high speed of support in order to maximise the potential to maintain possession.

5. Don't force the pass, but look to score and be positive when in possession.

BIBLIOGRAPHY

Chapter 1: Football Training and Practices

- Abrantes, C.I., Nunes, M.I., Maçãs, V.M., Leite, N.M., & Sampaio, J.E. (2012). Effects of the number of players and game type constraints on heart rate, rating of perceived exertion, and technical actions of small-sided football games. J Strength Cond Res, 26 (4): 976–981.

- Aguiar M., Botelho G., Lago C., Maças V., Sampaio J. (2012). A Review on the Effects of Football Small-Sided Games, 103-113.

- Arnason A., Sigurdsson SB., Gudmundsson A., Holme I., Engebretsen L., Bahr R. (2004). Physical fitness, injuries, and team performance in football. Med Sci Sports & Exercise, 36 (2): 278-285.

- Breil FA., Weber SN., Koller S., Hoppeler H., Vogt M. (2010). Block training periodization in alpine skiing: effects of 11-day HIT on VO2max and performance. Eur J Appl Physiol, 109 (6): 1077-1086.

- Buchheit M., Al Haddad H., Millet GP., Lepretre PM., Newton M., Ahmaidi S. (2009). Cardiorespiratory and Cardiac Autonomic Responses to 30-15 Intermittent Fitness Test in Team Sport Players. J Strength Cond Res, 23 (1): 93-100.

- Casamichana D., Castellano J. (2010). Time–motion, heart rate, perceptual and motor behaviour demands in small-sides football games: Effects of pitch size. J Sports Sci, 28 (14): 1615-1623.

- Chagovets NR. (1956). Biochemical changes in the muscles during rest after physical effort. Ukr Bioch Journ, 29: 450-457.

- Coutts AJ., Rampinini E., Marcora SM., Castagna C., Impellizzeri FM. (2009). Heart rate and blood lactate correlates of perceived exertion during small-sided football games. J Sci Med Sport, 12 (1) :79-84.

- Dellal, A., Chamari K., Owen A., Wong DP., Lago-Penas C., Hill-Haas S. (2011). Influence of the technical instructions on the physiological and physical demands within small-sided football games. Eur J Sport Sci, 11: 341–346.

- Dellal A., Diniz da Silva C., Hill-Haas S., Wong DP., Natali AJ., De Lima J., Bara Filho M., Marins J., Garcia ES., Chamari K. (2012). Heart Rate Monitoring in Football: Interest and Limits During Competitive Match Play and Training, Practical Application. J Strength Con Res 26 (10): 2890-2906.

- Dellal A., Wong DP. (2013). Repeated sprint and change-of-direction abilities in football players: effects of age group. J Strength Cond Res, 27 (9): 2504-2508.

- Fanchini M., Azzalin A., Castagna C., Schena F., McCall A., Impellizzeri FM. (2011). Effect of bout duration on exercise intensity and technical performance of small-sided games in football. J Strength Cond Res, 25: 453-458.

- Gabbett TJ., Mulvey MJ. (2008). Time-motion analysis of small-sided training games and competition in elite women football players. J Strength Con Res, 22: 543-552.

- Harre D. (1983). Principles of Sports Training. Berlin: Sportverlag, Germany.

- Hill-Haas SV., Coutts AJ., Rowsell GJ., Dawson BT. (2009). Generic versus small-sided game training in football. Int J Sports Med, 30 (9): 636-642.

- Hill-Haas SV., Dawson B., Impellizzeri FM., Coutts AJ. (2011). Physiology of small-sided games training in football: A systematic review. Sports Med, 41: 199–220.

- Hoff J., Helgerud J. (2004). Endurance and strength training for football players. Physiological considerations. Sports Med, 34: 165–80.

- Issurin VB. (2010). New horizons for the methodology and physiology of training periodization. Sports Med, 40 (3): 189-206.

- Issurin V., Kaverin V. (1985). Planirovainia i Postroenie Godovogo Cikla Podgotovki Grebcov. Moscow: Grebnoj port.

- Jan van Winckel. Fitness in football – the science

- Jones S., Drust B. (2007). Physiological and technical demands of 4 vs. 4 and 8 vs. 8 in elite youth football players. Kinesiol, 39:150-156.

- Kelly DM., Drust B. (2009). The effect of pitch dimensions on heart rate responses and technical demands of small-sided football games in elite players. J Sci Med Sport; 12: 475-479.

- Köklü Y., Ersöz G., Alemdaroglu U., Asç A., Özkan A. (2012). Physiological Responses and Time-Motion Characteristics of 4-A-Side Small-Sided Game in Young Football Players: The Influence of Different Team Formation Methods. J Strength Cond Res, 26 (11): 3118-3123.

- Le Meur Y., Hausswirth & Mujika (2012). Tapering for competition: A review, Science & Sport.

- Mallo J. (2012). Effect of block periodization on physical fitness during a competitive football season. Int J Perf Analy Sport,12 (1): 64-74

- Mallo J., Navarro E. (2008). Physical load imposed on football players during small-sided training games. J Sports Med Phys Fitness, 48: 166-171

- Matveyev L. (1981). Fundamentals of Sports Training. Moscow: Fizkultura i Sport, 1977; Moscow: Progress, 1981 [translated by A.P. Zdornykh]; pp. 245-259).

- Matveyev, 1964 - Periodization

- Owen A., Wong DP., McKenna M., Dellal A. (2011). Heart rate response and technical comparison between small- vs. large-sided games in elite professional football. J Strength Con Res, 25 (8): 2104-2110.

- Owen A., Wong D., Dellal A. (2012). Effects of a periodized small-sided game training intervention on physical performance in elite professional football. J Strength Con Res, 26 (10): 2748–2754.

- Platonov V. (1997). The general of the theory of preparation of sportsmen in Olympic sport.

- Olympic literature, Kyiv (in Russian).

- Rampinini E., Impellizzeri FM., Castanga C., Abt G., Chamari K., Sassi A., Marcora SM. (2007). Factors influencing physiological responses to small-sided football games. J Sports Sci, 25: 659–666.

- Reilly, T. (2005). An ergonomics model of the football training process. J Sports Sci, 23 (6): 561-572.

- Saltin B., Essen B. (1971). Muscle glycogen, lactate, ATP, and CP in intermittent exercise. In Muscle metabolism during exercise, pages 419-424. Springer US.

- Terjung RL., Baldwin KM., Winder WW., Holloszy JO. (1974). Glycogen repletion in different types of muscle and in liver after exhausting exercise. Am J Physiol, 226: 1387–1391.

- Yakovlev NN. (1955). Survey on sport biochemistry [in Russian]. Moscow: FiS Publisher.

- Zimkin 1961 – Periodization.

- Zheliazkov, 1981 - Periodization.

Chapter 2: Small Sided Games

- Abrantes, C.I., Nunes, M.I., Maçãs, V.M., Leite, N.M., & Sampaio, J.E. (2012). Effects of the number of players and game type constraints on heart rate, rating of perceived exertion, and technical actions of small-sided soccer games. J Strength Cond Res, 26 (4): 976–981.

- Aguiar M., Botelho G., Lago C., Maçãs V., Sampaio J. (2012). A Review on the Effects of Soccer Small-Sided Games, 103-113.

- Arnason A., Sigurdsson SB., Gudmundsson A., Holme I., Engebretsen L., Bahr R. (2004). Physical fitness, injuries, and team performance in soccer. Med Sci Sports & Exercise, 36 (2): 278-285.

- Barros RML., Misuta MS., Menezes RP. (2007). Analysis of the distances covered by first division Brazilian soccer players obtained with an automatic tracking method. J Sports Sci Med, 6 (2): 233-42.

- Bloomfield, J., Ploman, R., O'Donoghue, P. (2007). Physical Demands of Different Positions in FA Premier League Soccer. Sport Sci Med, Mar 1; 6 (1): 63-70.

- Breil FA., Weber SN., Koller S., Hoppeler H., Vogt M. (2010). Block training periodization in alpine skiing: effects of 11-day HIT on VO2max and performance. Eur J Appl Physiol, 109 (6): 1077-1086.

- Brito, J., Hertzog, M., & Nassis G.P. (2015). Do match-related contextual variables influence training load in highly trained soccer players?

- Bradley PS, Sheldon W, Wooster B, Olsen, P., Boanas, P., & Krustrup, P. (2009) High-intensity running in English FA Premier League soccer matches. J Sports Sci, 27: 159–168.

- Bradley, P.S., Carling, C., Archer, D., Roberts, J., Dodds, A., Di Mascio, M., Paul, D., Gomez Diaz, A., Peart, D., Krustrup, P. (2011). The effect of playing formation on high-intensity running and technical profiles in English FA Premier League soccer matches. J Sports Sci 2011 ; 9 : 821 – 830.

- Buchheit M., Al Haddad H., Millet GP., Lepretre PM., Newton M., Ahmaidi S. (2009). Cardiorespiratory and Cardiac Autonomic Responses to 30-15 Intermittent Fitness Test in Team Sport Players. J Strength Cond Res, 23(1):93-100.

- Buchheit, M., Allen, A., Poon, T.K., Modonutti, M., Gregson, W., & Di Salvo, V. (2014). Integrating different tracking systems in football: multiple camera semi-automatic system, local position measurement and GPS technologies. J Sports Sci, 32, 1844-1857.

- Carling, C., Bloomfield, J., Nelsen, L., Reilly, T. (2008). The role of motion analysis in elite soccer contemporary performance measurement techniques and work rate data . Sports Med, 38: 839 – 862.

- Casamichana D., Castellano J. (2010). Time–motion, heart rate, perceptual and motor behaviour demands in small-sides soccer games: Effects of pitch size. J Sports Sci, 28 (14): 1615-1623.

- Chagovets NR. (1956). Biochemical changes in the muscles during rest after physical effort. Ukr Bioch Journ, 29: 450-457.

- Coutts AJ., Rampinini E., Marcora SM., Castagna C., Impellizzeri FM. (2009). Heart rate and blood lactate correlates of perceived exertion during small-sided soccer games. J Sci Med Sport, 12 (1): 79-84.

- Coutts, A. J., Chamari, K., Impellizzeri, F. M., & Rampinini, E. (2008). Monitoring Training in Soccer: Measuring and Periodising Training. In D. Alexandre (Ed.), De l'entraînement à la performance en football (pp. 242–258). Bruxelles: de Boeck.

- Dawson B. (1996). Periodisation of speed and endurance training. In P. R. J. Reaburn & D. G. Jenkins (Eds.), Training for Speed and Endurance (pp. 76-96). Sydney: Allen & Unwin.

- Dellal, A., Wong, D. P., Moalla, W., & Chamari, K. (2010). Physical and technical activity of soccer players in the French First League-with special reference to their playing position. Int J Sports Med; 11: 278–290.

- Dellal, A., Chamari K., Owen A., Wong DP., Lago-Penas C., Hill-Haas S. (2011). Influence of the technical instructions on the physiological and physical demands within small-sided soccer games. Eur J Sport Sci, 11: 341–346.

- Dellal A., Diniz da Silva C., Hill-Haas S., Wong DP., Natali AJ., De Lima J., Bara Filho M., Marins J., Garcia ES., Chamari K. (2012). Heart Rate Monitoring in Soccer: Interest and Limits During Competitive Match Play and Training, Practical Application. J Strength Con Res 26 (10): 2890-2906.

- Dellal A., Wong DP. (2013). Repeated sprint and change-of-direction abilities in soccer players: effects of age group. J Strength Cond Res, 27 (9): 2504-2508.

- Di Mascio, M., & Bradley, P.S.(2012) Evaluation of the most intense high-intensity running period in English FA premier league soccer matches. J Strength Cond Res. Apr; 27(4):909-15 Di Salvo, V., Collins, A., McNeill, B., Cardinale, M. (2006). Validation of Prozone: A new video-based performance analysis system. Int J Perf Anal Sport. 6: 108 – 109.

- Di Salvo. W., Pigozzi, F., González-Haro, C., Laughlin, M.S., De Witt, J.K. (2013) Match Performance Comparison in Top English Soccer Leagues. Int J Sports Med; 34: 526–532.

- Eirale, C., Tol, J.L., Farooq, A., Farooq, A., Smiley, F., & Chalabi, H. (2013). Low injury rate correlates with team success in Qatari professional football. Br J Sports Med, 47: 807–8.

- Fanchini M., Azzalin A., Castagna C., Schena F., McCall A., Impellizzeri FM. (2011). Effect of bout duration on exercise intensity and technical performance of small-sided games in soccer. J Strength Cond Res, 25: 453-458.

- Foster, C. (1998). Monitoring training in athletes with reference to overtraining syndrome. Medicine and Science in Sports and Exercise, 30: 1164-1168.

- Foster, C, Florhaug, JA, Franklin, J, Gottschall, L, Hrovatin, LA, Parker, S, Doleshal, P, and Dodge, C. (2001). A new approach to monitoring exercise training.J Strength Cond Res15: 109–115.

- Gabbett TJ., Mulvey MJ. (2008). Time-motion analysis of small-sided training games and competition in elite women soccer players. J Strength Con Res, 22: 543-552.

- Gamble P. (2006). Periodization of training for team sports athletes. Strength Cond J, 28 (5): 56-66.

- Harre D. (1983). Principles of Sports Training. Berlin: Sportverlag, Germany.

- Hill-Haas SV., Coutts AJ., Rowsell GJ., Dawson BT. (2009). Generic versus small-sided game training in soccer. Int J Sports Med, 30 (9): 636-642.

- Hill-Haas SV., Dawson B., Impellizzeri FM., Coutts AJ. (2011). Physiology of small-sided games training in football: A systematic review. Sports Med, 41: 199–220.

- Hoff J., Helgerud J. (2004). Endurance and strength training for soccer players. Physiological considerations. Sports Med, 34: 165–80.

- Impellizzeri, F.M., Marcora, S.M., Castagna, C., Reilly, T., Sassi, A., Iaia, F.M., and Rampinini, E. Physiological and performance effects of generic versus specific aerobic training in soccer players. Int J Sports Med. 27 (6): 483-92. 2006.

- Impellizzeri, F. M., Rampinini, E., Coutts, A. J., Sassi, A., & Marcora, S. M. (2004). Use of RPE-based training load in soccer. Med Sci Sports Exerc, 36,1042–1047.

- Issurin V. (2010). New horizons for the methodology and physiology of training periodization. Sports Med, 40 (3): 189-206.

- Issurin V., Kaverin V. (1985). Planirovainia i Postroenie Godovogo Cikla Podgotovki Grebcov. Moscow: Grebnoj port.

- Van Winckel, J., Tenney, D., Helsen, W., McMillan, K., Meert, J.P., Bradley, P. (2014). Fitness in Soccer: The science and practical application, Moveo Ergo Sum / Leuven.

- Jennings, D., Cormack, S., Coutts, A. J., Boyd, L., & Aughey, R. J. (2010). The validity and reliability of GPS units for measuring distance in team sport specific running patterns. Int J Sports Physiol Perform, 5, 328-341.

- Jeong, T.S., Reilly, T., Morton, J., Bae, S.W., & Drust, B. (2011).Quantification of the physiological loading of one week of "pre-season" and one week of "in-season" training in professional soccer players. J Sports Sci, 29 (11): 1161-1166.

- Jones S., Drust B. (2007). Physiological and technical demands of 4 vs. 4 and 8 vs. 8 in elite youth soccer players. Kinesiol, 39: 150-156.

- Kelly DM., Drust B. (2009). The effect of pitch dimensions on heart rate responses and technical demands of small-sided soccer games in elite players. J Sci Med Sport; 12: 475-479.

- Kelly VG., Coutts AJ. (2007). Planning and monitoring training loads during the competition phase in team sports. Strength Cond J, 29 (4): 32-37.

- Köklü Y., Ersöz G., Alemdaroglu U., Asç A., Özkan A. (2012). Physiological Responses and Time-Motion Characteristics of 4-A-Side Small-Sided Game in Young Soccer Players: The Influence of Different Team Formation Methods. J Strength Cond Res, 26 (11): 3118-3123.

- Lago, C. (2009) The influence of match location, quality of opposition, and match status on possession strategies in professional association football . J Sports Sci ; 27: 1463–1469.

- Le Meur Y., Hausswirth & Mujika (2012). Tapering for competition: A review, Science & Sport.

- MacLeod H, Morris J, Nevill A, Sunderland C. (2009) The validity of a non-differential global positioning system for assessing player movement patterns in field hockey. J Sports Sci.27: 121–128.

- Mallo, J., Dellal, A. (2013). Injury risk in professional football players with special reference to the playing position and training periodization. Inj Prev. 2014 Aug; 20(4):e8. doi: 10.1136/injuryprev-2013-041092. Epub 2013 Dec 13.

- Mallo J. (2012). Effect of block periodization on physical fitness during a competitive soccer season. Int J Perf Analy Sport, 12 (1): 64-74.

- Mallo J., Navarro E. (2008). Physical load imposed on soccer players during small-sided training games. J Sports Med Phys Fitness, 48: 166-171.

- Malone, J., Di Michele, R., Morgans, R., Burgess, D., Morton, J.P., & Drust, B. (2015). Seasonal training load quantification in elite English Premier League soccer players. Int J Sports Physiol Perform, 10,489-497.

- Matveyev L. (1981). Fundamentals of Sports Training. Moscow: Fizkultura i Sport, 1977; Moscow: Progress, 1981 [translated by A.P. Zdornykh]; pp. 245-259.

- Matveyev, L.P. (1964). Problem of periodization the sport training. [In Russian.] Moscow: FiS Publisher.

- McMillan. K., Helgerud. J., Grant, S.J., Newell, J., Wilson, J., Macdonald, R., & Hoff, J. (2005) Lactate threshold responses to a season of professional British youth soccer. Br J Sports Med, 39: 432-436.

- Mohr, M., Krustrup, P., & Bangsbo, J. (2003) Match performance of high standard soccer players with special reference to development of fatigue. J Sports Sci; 21: 519-528.

- Osgnach, C., Poser, S., Bernardini, R., Rinaldo, R., Di Prampero, P.E. (2010) Energy cost and metabolic power in elite soccer: a new match analysis approach. Med Sci Sports Exerc; 42: 170–178

- Owen A., Wong DP., McKenna M., Dellal A. (2011). Heart rate response and technical comparison between small- vs. large-sided games in elite professional soccer. J Strength Con Res, 25 (8): 2104-2110.

- Owen, A, Wong, D.P., Paul, D., Dellal, A. (2012). Effects of a periodized small-sided game training intervention on physical performance in elite professional soccer. J Strength Cond Res. Oct; 26 (10): 2748-54.

- Owen, A., Wong, D.P., Paul, D.J., Orhant, E., Collie, S. (2013). Effect of an injury prevention program on muscle injuries in elite professional soccer. J Strength Cond Res. Dec; 27 (12): 3275-85.

- Owen, A., Wong, D.P., Paul, D., Dellal, A. (2014). Physical and technical comparisons between various-sided games within professional soccer. Int J Sports Med, Apr; 35 (4): 286-92

- Platonov V. (1997). The general of the theory of preparation of sportsmen in Olympic sport. Olympic literature, Kyiv (in Russian).

- Rampinini, E., Coutts, A.J., Castagna, C., Sassi, R., & Impellizzeri F.M. (2007) Variation in top level soccer match performance. Int J Sports Med, 28: 1018-1024.

- Rampinini E., Impellizzeri FM., Castanga C., Abt G., Chamari K., Sassi A., Marcora SM. (2007). Factors influencing physiological responses to small-sided soccer games. J Sports Sci, 25:659–666.

- Randers MB., Mujika I., Hewitt A., Santisteban J., Bischoff R., Solano R. (2010). Application of four different football match analysis systems: A comparative study. J Sport Sci, 28: 171–182.

- Reilly, T. (2005). An ergonomics model of the soccer training process. J Sports Sci, 23 (6): 561-572.

- Reilly T. The training process. In: Reilly T, ed. The Science of Training—Soccer: A Scientific Approach to Developing Strength, Speed and Endurance. London: Routledge; 2007:1–19.

- Rodríguez-Marroyo, J.A., & Antoñan C. (2015). Validity of the Session Rating of Perceived Exertion for Monitoring Exercise Demands in Youth Soccer Players. Int J Sports Physiol Perform, 10,404-407.

- Saltin B., Essen B. (1971). Muscle glycogen, lactate, ATP, and CP in intermittent exercise. In Muscle metabolism during exercise, p419-424. Springer US.

- Scott, B.R., Lockie, R.G., Knight, T.J., Clark, A.C., de Jonge, J. (2012). A comparison of methods to quantify the in-season training load of professional soccer players. J Sports Med Phys Fitness. Dec; 52 (6): 631-8.

- Strudwick T., Reilly T. (2001). Work-rate profiles of elite Premier League football players. Insight, 2 (2): 28-29.

- Terjung RL., Baldwin KM., Winder WW., Holloszy JO. (1974). Glycogen repletion in different types of muscle and in liver after exhausting exercise. Am J Physiol, 226: 1387–1391.

- Vigne, G., Dellal, A., Gaudino, C., Chamari, K., Rogowski, I., Alloatti, G., Wong, P.D., Owen, A., Hautier, C. (2013). Physical outcome in a successful Italian Serie A soccer team over three consecutive seasons. J Strength Cond Res. May; 27 (5): 1400-6.

- Yakovlev NN. (1955). Survey on sport biochemistry [in Russian]. Moscow: FiS Publisher.

CPSIA information can be obtained
at www.ICGtesting.com
Printed in the USA
FSOW04n2121081216
28358FS